DIAMOND HEART

Book One

OTHER BOOKS BY A. H. ALMAAS

Essence with The Elixir of Enlightenment
The Diamond Approach to Inner Realization

Facets of Unity
The Enneagram of Holy Ideas

Luminous Night's Journey
An Autobiographical Fragment

Work on Superego

DIAMOND MIND SERIES

Volume I: The Void
Inner Spaciousness and Ego Structure

Volume II: The Pearl Beyond Price
*Integration of Personality into Being:
An Object Relations Approach*

Volume III: The Point of Existence
*Transformations of Narcissism
in Self-Realization*

DIAMOND HEART SERIES

Book One: Elements of the Real in Man
Book Two: The Freedom to Be
Book Three: Being and the Meaning of Life
Book Four: Indestructible Innocence

DIAMOND HEART

Book One

Elements of the Real in Man

A. H. Almaas

Shambhala
Boston & London
2000

Shambhala Publications
Horticultural Hall
300 Massachusetts Avenue
Boston, Ma. 02115
www.shambhala.com

9 8 7 6 5 4 3 2 1

First Shambhala Edition
Printed in the United States of America

⊛ This edition is printed on acid-free paper that meets
the American National Standards Institute Z39.48 Standard.
Distributed in the United States by Random House, Inc.,
and in Canada by Random House of Canada Ltd

For the permission to reprint selected material, the author is grateful to
the following:
Jonathan Cape Ltd. for *Thinkers of the East*, Idries Shah, 1971; E.P. Dut-
ton, a division of the New American Library, for *Tales of the Dervishes*,
Idries Shah, 1970, copyright © 1967 by Idries Shah; Beacon Press for *The
Kabir Book*, versions by Robert Bly, copyright © 1971, 1977 by Robert
Bly, copyright © 1977 by the Seventies Press; "Is That So?" from *Zen
Flesh, Zen Bones* compiled by Paul Reps, Anchor Books, Doubleday and
Company, New York.

Library of Congress Cataloging-in-Publication Data
Almaas, A. H.
Elements of the real in man / A. H. Almaas.— 1st Shambhala ed.
p. cm.— (Diamond heart; bk. 1)
Originally published: Berkeley, Calif.: Diamond Books, 1987.
(Diamond heart; bk. 1)
ISBN 0-936713-01-1 (pbk.: alk. paper)
1. Conduct of life. 2. Self-realization. I. Title.
BJ1581.2.A42 2000
158.1—dc21
00–040028

Inside this clay jug there are canyons and pine mountains,
    and the maker of canyons and pine mountains!
All seven oceans are inside, and hundreds of millions
    of stars.
The acid that tests gold is there, and the one who judges
    jewels.
And the music from the strings no one touches,
    and the source of all water.

If you want the truth, I will tell you the truth:
Friend, listen: the God whom I love is inside.

— Kabir
from *The Kabir Book*
versions by Robert Bly

TABLE OF CONTENTS

PREFACE

We live in a world of mystery, wonder, and beauty. But most of us seldom participate in this real world, being aware rather of a world that is mostly strife, suffering, or meaninglessness. This situation is basically due to our not realizing and living our full human potential. This potential can be actualized by the realization and development of the human essence. The human essence is the part of us that is innate and real, and can participate in the real world.

This Diamond Heart series of books is a transcription of talks I have given to inner work groups in both California and Colorado, for several years, as part of the work of these groups. The purpose of the talks is to guide and orient individuals who are intensely engaged in doing the difficult work of essential realization.

The talks are organized in a manner that shows the various states and stages of realization in the order that occurs for the typical student, at least in our teaching method: the Diamond Approach. They begin with the states, knowledge, and questions most needed for starting the work on oneself, proceeding to stages of increasing depth and subtlety, and culminating in detailed understanding of the most mature states and conditions of realization.

Each talk elucidates a certain state of Essence or Being. The relevant psychological issues and barriers are discussed precisely and specifically, using modern psychological understanding in relation to the state of Being, and in relation to one's mind, life, and process of inner unfoldment.

Hence, this series is not only a detailed and specific guidance for the student, but also an expression and manifestation of the unfoldment of the human essence as it reveals the mystery, wonder, exquisiteness, and richness of the real world, our true inheritance. Each talk is actually the expression of a certain aspect or dimension of Being as it descends into the consciousness of the teacher in response to the present needs of the students. The teacher acts both as an embodiment of such reality and as a channel for the living knowledge that is part of this embodiment.

It is my wish that more of my fellow human beings participate in our real world, and taste the incredible beauty and integrity of being a human being, a full manifestation of the love of the truth.

Richmond, California 1986

ONE

In the World
But Not of It

There is a Sufi saying, "to be in the world but not of it." This phrase can have many meanings. The meaning depends on the situation and on your own development and capacity for understanding. To be "in the world but not of it" is a matter of orientation. I will talk about some of the meanings of this phrase so you will have a better understanding of what we are doing here.

When a baby is born, it is pretty much all Essence or pure Being. Its essence is not, of course, the same as the essence of a developed or realized adult. It is a baby's essence—non-differentiated, all in a big bundle. As the infant grows, the personality starts developing through interactions with the environment, especially the parents. Since most parents are identified with their personalities and not with their essence,

1

they do not recognize or encourage the essence of the child. After a few years, Essence is forgotten, and instead of Essence, there is now personality. Essence is replaced with various identifications. The child identifies with one or the other parent, with this or that experience, and with all kinds of notions about itself. These identifications, experiences, and notions become consolidated and structured as the personality. The child and, later, the adult believes this structure is its true self.

Essence was there in the beginning, and it is still there. Although it was not seen, not recognized, and was even rejected and hurt in many ways, it is still there. In order to protect itself, it has gone underground, undercover. The cover is the personality.

There is nothing bad about having a personality. You have to have one. You couldn't survive without it. However, if you take the personality to be who you truly are, then you are distorting reality because you are not your personality. The personality is composed of experiences of the past, of ideas, of notions, of identifications. You have the potential to develop a real individuality, the Personal Essence, which is different from the personality that covers the loss of Essence, but this potential is usually taken over by what we call our ego, our acquired sense of identity.

If a person believes himself to be the ego, resulting from identifications, ideas and past experiences, then he is said to be "not in the world, but of it." He is not aware of who he really is, of his essence. This is difficult to understand unless we are aware of our own essence, at least some of the time.

The ego, or the sense of ego identity, takes the place of what we call the real identity, and the personality as a whole takes the place of Essence. The personality is a substitute, an impostor. The world is the same for both Essence and personality, but the way the world is seen is different.

A person who is "not in the world, but of it," is oriented toward the personality instead of toward Essence.

Let's give a few examples of how being identified with your personality distorts reality and results in suffering. Let's take the issue of proving yourself in the world, of being independent, on your own, strong, successful, making a place for yourself. That's a big concern, a major pre-occupation. Nearly everyone has this goal. This can be an aim that comes from an essential orientation or a personality orientation. There is a big, big difference. Establishing yourself in the world and being independent means building the personal aspect of Essence. It is an inner accomplishment. It comes from a very deep desire to actualize who you really are. Being who you really are means being free of all the identifications from the past that have built your false sense of identity; it does not depend on what you do in the world. What you do in the world can be an expression of who you are, but it does not define you. When you are your Personal Essence, your own true sense of identity, anything you do will have an essential orientation. You usually think that the job you choose, whatever it is—gardener, physicist, mother—will make you feel who you really are. But that means you are identified with being a part of the world. It means there is a distortion of reality.

Usually when a person is beginning to work on herself, she has no idea of the difference between choices that are motivated by personality and choices motivated by Essence. She may think that doing this kind of thing instead of that kind of thing will help her be herself, but there is no clear guiding principle. The person not only lacks a guiding principle, but because of ego identifications, she believes what her personality is urging her to do and is very vehement about defending these things. "This is me. This is who I am. This is what is best to do." Every time you question her plans for the future or her ideas about who she thinks she is, she feels threatened. To even begin to question these structures means the possibility of destroying all her beliefs.

In the Diamond Approach we say that the drive of the personality for independence and identity is really a distorted reflection of wanting a certain aspect of Essence—what we call the personal aspect. This is often referred to in certain Sufi stories as the Princess Precious Pearl or the Pearl Beyond Price. There are many stories about the princess—the Personal Essence—being liberated from a prison which is, of course, the prison of the personality, what is false in us. In other stories, it is the search for a precious gem that represents the search for Personal Essence.

How do you apply "in the world but not of it" to this situation? "Being in the world but not of it" means that you continue doing what you do. You continue to pursue your career as a physicist, a gardener, a mother and so on, but all the time you remember that it is only a reflection of something else, that what you most deeply want is to actualize a part of yourself. So the main effort is directed toward understanding that part of yourself and actualizing it. If you live that way, it is true that you are in the world, but your motivation is different. You are not *of* the world. Your purpose is not to be a physicist, a gardener, or a mother. Your purpose is find the precious pearl, your Personal Essence. If you're a physicist, you could be awarded one prize after another; if you're a lawyer, you could become the state attorney. Yet you will still feel unfulfilled if you haven't found the pearl. You'll still have to do more, try more, prove more. You could spend your life striving for bigger and better results.

Do not misinterpret what I'm saying. I'm not saying that you must not pursue what you're pursuing. I'm not saying that you must sit home and think about what the precious pearl is. I'm saying that whatever you're doing is a distortion of the real thing until your orientation is toward Essence and you have actualized the Personal Essence. Because your personality is a distortion of the real thing, it can point to the real thing. By understanding it, you can begin to see what the truth is in you that is being reflected.

The saying isn't "not of the world"; it is "in the world but not of it." When you are "in the world," you are not meditating on some mountain, not living in a monastery. You're actually living the life of the world. Your life is an adventure, and whatever you are doing in the world is not an end in itself but is a crucible for melting the ore into gold. Once you know yourself to be the Personal Essence, what you do doesn't much matter. You choose whatever will enlarge and enhance your real self. There can never be a sense of lasting fulfillment unless you have realized that essential part of yourself. Nothing else can take its place.

Let's take another example: the issue of being with somebody and remaining independent. Often, to be in a relationship, it seems you have to sacrifice part of yourself, to compromise. What if you don't want to do that? What if you want to be close, intimate, loved and loving, and still be yourself without compromising? How can you be "in the world but not of it" in this example? To answer that, we first need to understand something about the nature of relationships.

The core of the need for intimate love relationships is the desire to actualize a certain relationship you had in early childhood with your mother. When you were a baby, four or five months old, you were in a state called "symbiotic union." In this state, you were essentially merged with your mother. There was no sense of "I am me" and "you are someone else." There was total, nondifferentiated unity with wonderful, pleasurable, warm, melting kinds of sensations.

When you think about what you want in a relationship, you'll usually find that what you want is to be so close that there are no longer two separate individuals. There is a deep desire to melt into the other person, with no boundaries, so that it's not even a question of two people loving each other—there is just a state of love. It's a big puddle—a wonderful, golden puddle—like honey with the sun shining through it. A golden womb. You feel safe, protected, melting. Your body is all pleasure; your mind doesn't exist. Because we had this experience with mother during our infancy, we believe very deeply that to have this state again, we must be with another person. So, we search for the right person. What we are actually searching for is that sense of merging, the golden, melting feeling.

How can we have this and not be "of the world"? It is necessary to understand that the state of complete merging, of complete disappearance into a melted kind of pleasure, is a state of Essence. You do not have to be with someone else to have it. You can experience this aspect of Essence by yourself or with your cat, with the rug, with your car, with another person—anything. Our belief that we need somebody else in order to have this golden merged feeling is very strong. "If I could just melt into your arms, if you just loved me, everything would be wonderful." You think that's what will do it. For most people it is easier to experience the merged state with somebody else because they believe that having somebody else there is a precondition for feeling that state in themselves. But the search is really for a certain aspect of Essence. So, in this case, to be "in the world and not of it" doesn't mean you have to forget about relationships and go off to a cave someplace or to the north pole and merge with the icebergs. If you want to do this, that's fine; it doesn't really matter. What does matter is that whatever you're doing, whether you're in a relationship or not, you need to look inside yourself and find what the barriers are that prevent you from experiencing that part of you that can feel merged and melted no matter who you're with or where you are.

The desire for this essential state affects not only couple relationships but also the wish to have children; people want that merged state with a child. Also, when people are looking for beautiful landscapes and things like that, what they really want is to feel merged with what's around them and they believe they need to satisfy one condition or another for that to happen. So, relationships can be a crucible for discovering a certain golden essential substance inside.

I have given two examples that are intimately connected. The first example has to do with independence, with being yourself, and brings up the issue of identity—the personal aspect of Essence. The other example has to do with relationships and usually brings up a conflict between being a separate self and the experience of merging, which often makes you feel as if you are losing your identity.

If you pay attention to your actual situation in the world, which is a distorted reflection of the true state of affairs, you can find what is really there. Your career, interests, and relationships are important, but they are only important insofar as they lead you toward a deeper understanding of yourself. Otherwise they are irrelevant.

Nothing is really important but who you are, as the following story illustrates.

> The Zen master Hakuin was praised by his neighbors as one living a pure life.
>
> A beautiful Japanese girl whose parents owned a food store lived near him.
>
> Suddenly, without any warning, her parents discovered she was with child.
>
> This made her parents angry. She would not confess who the man was, but after much harassment at last named Hakuin.
>
> In great anger the parents went to the master. "Is that so?" was all he would say.

After the child was born it was brought to Hakuin. By this time he had lost his reputation, which did not trouble him, but he took very good care of the child. He obtained milk from his neighbors and everything else the little one needed.

A year later the girl-mother could stand it no longer. She told her parents the truth—that the real father of the child was a young man who worked in the fish market.

The mother and father of the girl at once went to Hakuin to ask his forgiveness, to apologize at length, and to get the child back again.

Hakuin was willing. In yielding the child, all he said was: "Is that so?"

(Paul Reps, *Zen Flesh, Zen Bones*, pp. 7–8.)

Things keep changing for Hakuin. At times he looks good; at times he looks bad.

It doesn't make any difference to him. It has nothing to do with who he is. Who he is remains the same. What happens around him is irrelevant. He is still who he really is.

Your essence is very intelligent, very generous. It has a way of throwing a conflict in front of you so that by looking at that conflict, you'll find out something you need to know. The situation that you are given is perfect in terms of timing, place, the people involved, your capacities, the capacities of the people around you, every detail. The situation is such that if you actually try to understand it, you'll understand something about your essence. The situation is not there to give you a hard time. You'll have a hard time if you look only at the manifestation, seeing the conflict itself as a difficulty. If you look at it from the perspective of ego, of identification, you'll suffer and continue to suffer. But if you see that you fell on your face and you're suffering because you tripped over something that was in your way, then you'll want to find out more about what that was, more about that barrier.

What we do here is look at the barriers that you bring to work on in this group. We dismantle them, analyze them, examine where they come from in terms of your childhood and your relationships and your life in the world now. From that material, we eventually get the real and precious metal—or the gems hidden inside it. That's why all that stuff was there. You think that by working on your issue of independence you'll finally be independent, you'll be able to support yourself, earn a lot of money, do what you want and all of that. That's all true, but it's not the most important factor. The most important aspect of working on any issue is for something inside you to develop. The rest will follow almost effortlessly.

So, we're talking about being "in the world but not of it." All of us here live in the world and do what everybody else does: we wear clothes, eat food, go to the grocery store, have a job, make love, fight, everything. However, our focus is different. We do not identify with the part of us that eats, shops, works, and so on. We learn to develop the capacity to be aware of what is happening but not to identify with it; we develop what we call awareness and disidentification. These are the most important things you need in order to do the work of understanding yourself. You have to be aware of what's happening inside of you and outside of you. The world is seen as a big classroom; the situations are classes where you can develop certain aspects of yourself, certain aspects of your essence. The whole world is a big university offering many classes: classes on sex, classes on work, relationships, dependence and independence, and so on.

Little by little, we become aware of our life with all of its conflicts and barriers without totally believing that this is all there is. The more we're able to pay attention and disidentify, the more we'll be able to see the real truth that is there like veins of gold in piles of rocks. The truth is the gold in the ore. Developing this capacity to pay attention and to disidentify at the same time ultimately leads us to experience our essence.

"In the world but not of it" not only describes the person who is free; it describes Essence itself. That's the deeper aspect. What is this world that we're "in but not *of*"? The world is a multitude of things, but the world as we perceive it is primarily made up of mental thoughts and images, emotions, and sensations. Everything that you know about the world and yourself depends on thoughts, images, emotions, and sensations. What else do you know? Ultimately, the world as you perceive it comes down to your sensations of the world, your emotions about it, and the mental images and thoughts you have. For instance, a tree is a tree, but what is it for you? A certain image in your mind, a feeling about it, sensations you feel when you touch it. If you're sitting in a chair, what is the chair in your direct experience? A sensation under your butt, right? An image in your mind, an idea that causes you to sit this way instead of another. That is the world.

Now, Essence is "in the world but not of it." It's not sensations, emotions, or mental events. Yet it is "in the world." It is like the gold in the rock. It is not the rock; it's *in* the rock. Essence is *in* the sensations, emotions, and mental events, but it's not any of them. Precious stones are in the earth, but they are not the earth itself. They are something else. So is Essence in you. It's not your flesh, not your emotions, not your thoughts. But it is embedded there. Essence is in you like the gold in the rock, like precious stones in the earth.

Since this is the case, you can do some exploring, some mining, in order to find it. You can dig in the body, in the emotions, and in the mental events to find the precious substance. For example, you can do bodywork to develop the sensitivity of your body. Then you might discover what is there, what Essence is. You might explore your emotions and your sensations until you become so aware of them that you see subtle discriminations. You see that what you were sure was an emotion is not an emotion. You see that what you thought was a physical sensation is not a physical sensation. It is close, but not really a physical sensation. Essence is like a physical something that is not of the physical body. It is like a physical existence of a different level, a different dimension.

There is a deeper meaning to "in the world but not of it." Once found, Essence goes through a development, an alchemical refinement, until it reaches its basic nature— the true nature of Essence, which is the nature of everything. It is my nature, but it is also your nature. It is the nature of birds, cats, trees, rocks, everything. It is not the rocks, not the cat, not your body, not you, not me. It is the inner nature of these. It is what allows these to exist. That real nature of Essence, the nature of everything, is what is sometimes called God.

God, the essence of the Essence, is everywhere. It is in the physical body, in sensations, in thoughts, in the animate and inanimate. It is in everything, but it is not these things. It's *in* them but not *of* them. So God, the essence of the Essence, is "in the world but not of it," and this is the deepest meaning of the phrase.

There is another important aspect of being "in the world but not of it" that I want to point out here. It is the recognition of what Essence is and what it is not. This involves recognizing and acknowledging that Essence is working in you, that it is a real factor operating in you.

Essence develops very quickly the moment it is seen and recognized. It thrives on recognition. If you don't recognize it, it stays dormant. The moment you recognize it, it starts growing. It feeds on light. This is very important for certain aspects of our Work here. We must recognize what factors actually contribute to our change and development.

Let's say you've been working on yourself for a year or two, coming to this group and dealing with issues in your life, and some changes start happening. It could be that your heart opens, or you get clearer. You might say, "Oh, my heart opened because I met this wonderful woman; she's so marvelous. My heart just opened to her, and it's been open ever since."

In this case, you don't give recognition to your essential work; you give it to something else. You give credit where it is not due. When you do that, you invalidate your work. You've done two years of work on understanding yourself, but you're saying it didn't do a thing. You think your openness, your expansiveness, the fullness happened because you met this wonderful woman. Or you say your kundalini opened because somebody gave you this massage, somebody worked on your sacrum in a particular way. You completely ignore the fact that for five years you've dealt with all kinds of emotions and that if you hadn't done this work, somebody could have rubbed your sacrum with sandpaper and you wouldn't have felt a thing.

Perhaps you get a cold at the same time you feel that your heart is open; you might decide your heart is open because of the cold. You give the credit to your cold instead of acknowledging four years of work. The cold is probably a resistance against further opening. Getting sick is a common resistance to expansion. When you fail to recognize the value and impact of your essential work, you deprive yourself of the possibility of that work continuing, giving you more understanding of truth.

It is very important to have this discriminating faculty not only in terms of orientation—what we talked about earlier—but also in terms of what the real influences are in your life. If you do not give credit where it is due, you invalidate what actually brought about the growth—your own work, your own capacity, your own essence.

I've seen that many of my friends have experienced their essence but did not understand what it was because most of the time they invalidated the work they had done. Every time they went on to something new, to some other spiritual study or discipline, to some other self-exploration, they would invalidate what they had just learned. They would throw out their understanding and what they had attained that was of value. Then they would have to start all over again. I was lucky; I didn't invalidate anything. Whenever I moved on to something else, I understood exactly what I learned from the earlier experience. I found that this makes quite an important difference.

Sometimes it's not easy to tell what's contributing to the understanding and clarity in your life. But if you can discern what it is that is contributing, you'll increasingly move towards your essence, because only Essence brings this about. If, on the other hand, you attribute your development to external things, you are not only making a mistake in judgment but are also slowing or stopping the process that has really contributed to your development. You're telling your essence, "You don't matter." And that's an attack on your essence. Invalidating your essence is an activity of your ego or superego.

From what I have observed, people often do not acknowledge what's really happening or what force is operating because there is something in them that resists seeing and experiencing Essence. It's not just a mistake in judgment; there is an active motivation behind it. It is a defensive function of the superego. Also you have practically no support or guidance from the world around you. When people don't recognize the actual force in you that is contributing to the changes in your life, it is because they are resisting the perception of that force in themselves. They do not want to see the truth, so they don't want to recognize it in you. In my own experience, it is important that

I know what is bringing about my development. "In the world but not of it" extends to seeing the real causes, the real forces, operating in whatever we do. Any questions or comments?

Student: Is it possible that some people have more Essence working in them than other people, even though they're completely unconscious of it?

AH: Yes, it happens. It's what Gurdjieff called stupid saints, which means Being with no knowledge.

S: Are other people attracted to them because they want that quality?

AH: Sure. Sometimes people are developed essentially without doing any work on themselves simply because they didn't get too squashed at the beginning.

S: Or their essence is more evident because of some accident or some talent.

AH: Essence has nothing to do with talent. A person can be very talented but, at the same time, completely identified with their personality. Essence is, as I have said, "in the world but not of it." Talent is part of the world. Essence can bring to fruition the potentialities of the talents that already exist, but being intelligent or not intelligent, or creative in one way or another, has nothing to do with Essence.

TWO

The Theory of Holes

Today we will discuss a fundamental idea used in our work here. It's called the Theory of Holes. Under usual circumstances, people are full of what we call "holes." What is a hole? A hole refers to any part of you that has been lost, meaning any part of you that you have lost consciousness of. Ultimately what we have lost awareness of is our essence. When we are not aware of our essence, it stops manifesting. Then we feel a sense of deficiency. So a hole is nothing but the absence of a certain part of our essence. It could be the loss of love, loss of value, loss of capacity for contact, loss of strength, any of the qualities of Essence. There are many of them. However to say we have lost parts of Essence does not mean they are gone forever; they are never gone forever. You are simply cut off from them.

Let's take, for example, the quality of value or self-esteem. When you are cut off from your value, the actual experience is a sense that there is a hole inside that feels empty. You feel a sense of deficiency, a sense of inferiority, and you want to fill this hole with value from the outside. You may try to use approval, praise, whatever. You try to fill the hole with fake value.

We walk around with lots of holes, but we usually aren't aware of them. We're usually aware of desires: "I want praise. I want to be successful. I want this person to love me. I want this or that experience." The presence of desires and needs indicates the presence of holes.

These holes originated during childhood, partly as a result of traumatic experiences or conflicts with the environment. Perhaps your parents did not value you. They didn't treat you as if your wishes or presence were important, didn't act in ways that let you know that you mattered. They ignored your essential value. Because your value was not seen or acknowledged (perhaps even attacked or discouraged), you got cut off from that part of you, and what was left was a hole, a deficiency.

When you relate to someone in a deep way, you fill your holes with the other person. Some of your holes get filled with what you believe you're getting from the other person. For example, you may feel valued because this person appreciates you. You don't know consciously that you're filling the hole with their appreciation. But when you are with that person, you feel valuable, and unconsciously you feel the other person is responsible for your value. Whatever this person is giving you feels like a part of you; it is part of the fullness that you experience.

Your unconscious does not see that part of the person that makes you feel valuable as separate; you see it as part of you. When the person dies or the relationship ends, you don't feel that you're losing that person; you feel you're losing whatever is filling the hole. You experience the loss of a part of yourself. That is why it is so painful. It feels like you're being cut and something is being taken out of you. That's what the wound and the pain are about—the hurt of loss. You may feel as if you lost your heart, your security, your strength, your will—whatever the person fulfilled for you. When you lose a person close to you, you feel whatever hole that person has filled.

That's one thing people are talking about when they say that we "fit" each other. Each person fits the other's holes. This fits into this hole, that fits into that hole. When two people live together, they may feel full and complete because they feel themselves as complementary; together they make a unified whole.

It is rare that another person fills all your holes. You have many people and activities in your life, and still they don't fill all your holes. There will be some holes left, and this keeps the dissatisfaction going. And, of course, holes don't get filled perfectly. The moment the other person changes a little or says something that makes you feel bad, you feel the hole again. "Oh, he doesn't think I'm worth anything after all." You feel angry and hurt because the hole is getting exposed. So the dissatisfaction continues because the person is not always filling your holes perfectly, especially if he's wanting you to fill his holes.

S: When you change relationships, or a person in your life changes, then there must be a change in the holes involved.

AH: Right. If there's any change, there's a jiggling around of holes. Some holes become empty and some get filled. The person has to adjust and find other ways to fill the holes. This usually means they have to deal with some of these holes. They have to feel their presence and maybe understand them.

So now you know why the loss of somebody who has been very close to you, very intimate with you, is so painful.

After being with this person a long time, you're so accustomed to the fit, you believe that other person is part of you. Losing the person is losing a part of yourself.

When you experience this loss and separation directly, you have the possibility of seeing that what was filling you wasn't really you. If you stay with the hurt and the pain of loss without trying to cover it with something else, it is possible that you will feel the emptiness. You will feel and see the hole. Then, if you allow yourself to feel the deficiency, the emptiness, you may find the essential part of you that will fill the hole from the inside, once and for all. It's not even filling; it is the elimination of the hole and the identifications with the deficiency. In that way, you regain part of yourself. You connect with the part of your essence that you lost and that you thought only somebody else could provide for you.

Most people feel a loss of self-esteem when a relationship ends, which is why I'm using the particular example of value. To begin exploring the loss, you can stay with that feeling and ask yourself, "How come I feel so worthless? How come I feel like a nothing just because that person isn't around any more? Why do I feel I'm so much less valuable?" If you stay with that feeling without trying to change it, just paying attention and trying to understand it, then you will experience the deficiency and the hole. If you understand the deficiency and its source, you might even remember the actual event or pattern of events that brought about your loss of value.

A hole is usually filled with the part of the personality that has the memory of what was lost, the situation that brought about the loss, and the hurts and conflicts associated with it. We have to go through the hurt at the deepest level and get close to the hole itself to see these memories. When we see the memory of what was lost, the aspect of Essence that was lost will start flowing again.

So, any deep loss is an opportunity to grow, to understand more about yourself, to experience holes that you believe can only be filled by someone else. Unfortunately, people usually defend like crazy against deeply feeling these losses. This is primarily to avoid feeling the hole. People don't know that the hole, the sense of deficiency, is a symptom of a loss of something deeper—the loss of Essence, which can be regained. They think the hole, the deficiency, is how they really are at the deepest level, and that there is nothing beyond it. They think something is wrong with them, but this feeling that something is wrong is an unconscious knowledge of the presence of the hole.

People will do anything to not feel the hole. They believe that if they get close to a hole, it will swallow them up. If they are coming up to the hole of love, for example, they might feel threatened by a devastating loneliness or emptiness. Other holes will bring up what feels like a threat of annihilation. No wonder we don't want to go near these holes! But in our work here we have seen a surprising thing: when we stop defending against feeling a hole, the actual experience is not painful. We simply experience empty space, the feeling that there is nothing there. Not a threatening nothingness, but a spaciousness, an allowing. This spaciousness allows Essence to emerge, and it is Essence and only Essence that can eliminate the hole, that deficiency, from the inside.

S: Can a hole manifest as anger?

AH: Yes. You might have anger as a result of a deficiency, especially as a defense against feeling a hole. Most feelings, specifically those that are automatic and compulsive, are the result of holes. When there are no holes, there are no such emotions. Sadness, hurt, jealousy, anger, hatred, fear— all of these are the result of holes. If you have no holes, you don't have these emotions. You have only Essence. That's why such emotions are sometimes called passions, false feelings, or pseudo-feelings.

Our whole society is set up to teach us that we should get the outside to fill our holes; we should get value, love, strength, and so on from outside. We talk about how wonderful it is to do things for other people, or to fall in love, or have a meaningful profession as if these activities are what give life meaning. We attribute the meaning to the person or thing we think is responsible for it rather than to Essence, which is really responsible. Our whole society is arranged so that people fill each other's holes. Civilization as we know it is built around filling holes. It is a product of the personality. It is also the home of the personality. It is what sustains and nourishes the personality.

S: Has it always been this way?

AH: I don't think so. I think it happened gradually. It took a while for the personality of civilization to become so dominant. The more mechanical we become, the more culture is a matter of filling holes. Many people say that in the past there was more love and presence, more recognition of reality, and that people were more in touch with their essence than they are now. You've heard of the Golden Age? In the Golden Age, people experienced their essence, no holes. The Silver Age began as Essence diminished and the holes began to appear. Then came the Bronze Age. Now we're in the Iron Age. It's the darkest and heaviest. Iron is nothing but defense. We can sometimes feel the quality of iron in our hardness and determination to protect ourselves. So this is one way of viewing the present time—all defenses against holes.

Allowing ourselves to tolerate the holes and go through them to the other side is more difficult now because everything in society is against this. Society is against Essence. Everybody around you, wherever you go, is trying to fill holes, and people feel very threatened if you don't try to fill your holes in the same way they do. When a person is not trying to fill his holes, it tends to make other people feel their own holes more.

It's becoming more and more difficult to do the Work, and the Work is becoming more and more needed. That is why it is important to have a group like this where there is a community of people involved in the task of self-understanding. You have the support of many people who are allowing themselves to feel the holes instead of filling them. It is very difficult—almost impossible—for one person alone to do this because everything in her environment is against it.

S: You said something about the connection between holes and emotions and that Essence doesn't have any emotions. I don't understand.

AH: If you understand your feelings, you'll get to your essence. But that doesn't mean that your feelings are your essence.

S: Does that mean that if I am my Essence all the time, then I won't feel anything?

AH: No, it doesn't mean that. There are real feelings, and there are pseudo-feelings. The pseudo-feelings are attempts to fill the hole, which is the absence of the real feelings.

S: So what's in the hole is a fake feeling?

AH: Yes. If you lose your value, for instance, if at some point you get cut off from it, there will be a hole left. The hole will be experienced as a sense of inferiority or a lack of self-esteem. But that is not a real feeling. It is the absence of the real feeling of value or self-esteem. This inferiority will often be covered by an attempt to feel superior as a defense. But that's not a real feeling either. It's an attempt to hide, a pseudo-feeling. If you get angry when somebody does or says something and you feel inferior, that again is a pseudo-feeling. All these pseudo-feelings are coming up because you are not in touch with your real value. They are compensations. They are real in the sense that you do feel them, but they are not real in the sense that they are a consequence of losing what is real. This is an important difference. When you have been cut off from a real feeling, something else tries to take its place: the emotions. By feeling the emotions, you can see what it is you lost and experience it. When you experience real value, you see it is very different from the pseudo-feelings that covered over the loss. Emotions are reactions, while essential states like Value are states of Being. They are not reactions to anything.

S: If you have pseudo-feelings, what's underneath them?

AH: In this case, what's beneath inferiority, superiority, anger, and hurt is Value, which is a certain aspect of Essence.

Have you read Plato? Remember the Platonic Ideas or the Platonic forms? Socrates said that nobody could ever teach you about the forms. The only way you can know them is by remembering them. You have a memory of them, although you may not be aware of it. By retrieving the memory, you come to the Idea. What you return to is not emotions; you return to your Essence. Essence is more real and more substantial than emotions. Essence is as real as your blood. It is not a reaction.

Some people are not only cut off from their Essence, they are cut off from their emotions, too. This makes them very far from themselves. They have only their thoughts, which are the results of the emotions. This is the way we lose ourselves and come to identify with our thoughts. First there is Essence, then the loss of Essence, then the resulting emotions, then the loss of the emotions or the conflict around them, which creates all kinds of thoughts. So understanding emotions can help untangle the knots of defenses that are attempts to avoid experiencing the holes. Emotions can point to where Essence has been lost.

Most people wonder, if you don't feel emotions, what will you feel? The more you feel Essence, the less you feel emotions. You will still have sensations, which will be deeper and stronger than before, but your emotions will not be deeper and stronger. An emotion is only a response of the nervous system, whereas Essence is not a response of the nervous system. There is something there filling you. Part of you is present.

Some people consider the essential aspects the "real feelings." But what people usually call feelings or emotions are not Essence. Love, Peace, Value, Strength, and Will are aspects of Essence. With Essence, instead of experiencing anger, you experience Strength. Instead of feeling superior or inferior, you experience Value. You experience yourself as a rounded presence that is full and powerful.

S: The Work fills up a lot of my holes, and between the times that we work here, I begin to feel panicky. However, I think the feeling of fullness that I have with the Work is qualitatively different than when I fill myself up with another person. Also, the work I do here gives me the safety to feel the emptiness. A lot of times the feeling of fullness that I have from the Work comes right after you have helped me feel safe enough to feel the hole.

AH: Yes. The situation of the Work here is a little more complicated than normal situations. What you do in the outside world, you could do with the Work. Many people do try to fill their holes by being here. But there is another side of it, which is that the Work itself is oriented toward experiencing the deficiencies and not just the fullness.

If the fullness comes from using the Work to fill your holes in the normal way, then you can treat the holes that come up in between sessions just like any others and see what you feel you have lost. You can try to experience the hole and understand it.

People often use the Work to fill a certain hole, a certain deficiency. You might feel, "I'm with a group of intelligent, sincere, truth-seeking people; I must be wonderful." Later, you go home and then feel, "Maybe I'm not so wonderful after all." If so, let yourself experience that hole to understand it.

Some other kinds of processes in our Work can lead you to feel full because of the presence of a certain real fullness that gets you in touch with your own fullness. After a week when you're not in touch with it as deeply, you may question it. That's a different process. Maybe you felt full without understanding what happened, or perhaps there are other issues that must be exposed and worked through for you to keep the fullness.

The fullness of the Work is not the same as the fullness people experience by filling holes. The experience of filling a hole is not usually experienced as a fullness, really. When somebody is filling your holes, it feels shaky and not really satisfying. It feels like a temporary kind of relief. There is a sense of grabbiness, of holding; you don't want the other person to leave. You don't want them to change the way they behave towards you. At a deep level, it's actually a blockage, not an openness. The fullness of the Work is the absence of blockage.

Sometimes a lot of holes come up at once, so it's a little confusing. Usually, when somebody first comes to do the Work in the group, many holes are experienced at the same time. The purpose of the Work is to expose holes and let the person deal with these holes from within. We're not trying to fill holes from outside.

We could easily do all kinds of things to give people wonderful experiences here. We could do meditations and certain exercises, and everybody could feel wonderful things. However these will not last unless the person actually confronts his deficiencies, his holes, and goes through them. It is not a simple process, nor a short or easy one. It takes time and a lot of effort. To experience a hole and not act from the deficiency, is very difficult because of the powerful drive to fill it. You sometimes feel as if it is a matter of life and death.

S: This morning when I was eating breakfast out, I was realizing what a big hole the waitress filled.

AH: Yes. Many people earn their livings by filling other people's holes. Many businesses are there to fill people's holes. I have no moralistic attitude about filling holes. I don't think it is a sin. I don't think you should feel guilty about it or punish yourself for filling holes. Sometimes you fill your holes; sometimes you fill someone else's. So what? I prefer to try to understand whatever is there. I'm not building a religion saying, "Thou shalt not fill holes."

You can look at everything you do in terms of holes or filling holes. You will see that all the time you're either filling a hole, tolerating a hole, or experiencing the real thing that was lost. This is going on all the time, at every moment.

In this Work, the holes you deal with get bigger and bigger. First, you encounter the smaller holes, and then the bigger holes, until you get to the biggest hole of them all, which is the loss of everything. It's called death. When you die, you lose everything. So one of the last holes is the loss of the body itself. Physical death is like a big hole—a black, dark, empty hole with nothing in it. You try to fill that hole with the body. If you let the body go, at least in your consciousness—I don't mean that you necessarily die physically—then you'll suddenly see the complete you, the one you usually try to substitute your body for.

Most people think they are their bodies. It is one of our deepest identifications. That is one reason why we have cravings for physical pleasures. I think the basis for the deepest craving, the craving for physical pleasure, is a hole. The hole is the cutting off from the real pleasures, the essential pleasures. It is an absence.

Of course, nobody wants to believe that. "If I let go of that one, what will be left for me? If I don't eat cookies twice a day, have sex every other day, and do this and that, how am I going to enjoy myself?" This is one of the last holes to be explored.

The Work is not about changing yourself. You do whatever you do in your life and just study what's happening. That's all you need to do: Study your life to understand it. One of the ways the Work was done in the past was to retire into a monastery and renounce everything. The point was not really to reject everything; it was an attempt to experience holes. In time, such practices took on a moralistic tone—the feeling that it's bad to have certain kinds of external contact. The purpose of such retreats is to allow yourself to feel the holes and not fill them so you can see what they are all about.

I remember a diagram by Meher Baba. In this diagram, he was trying to demonstrate that God is everything, and for that everything to be complete, it has to have a nothing as part of it. And from that nothing, the world comes. He says all that we know is the result of the nothing that is in the everything. And we have to see that nothing in order to be able to know everything. So you must have a nothing, otherwise you won't be complete. Complete means you have everything, and everything includes a nothing.

One more thing about the theory of holes. As I said, the holes get produced when you're a child. When you're a baby, you have no holes; you are complete when you are born. As you grow up, because of your interactions with your environment and certain difficulties you encounter, you get cut off from certain parts of yourself. Every time you get cut off from a part of you, a hole manifests. The holes then become full with the memory of the loss and the issues around the loss. After a while, you fill in the holes. What you fill the holes with are false feelings, ideas, beliefs about yourself, and strategies for dealing with your environment. These fillers are collectively called the personality, or what we call the *false pearl*.

So the false pearl is a result of losses of parts of the self. After a time, we think this is who we are. We think we are the fillers. The personality is trying to take the place of the real thing. That's why we do a lot of work here on understanding our personalities. We study the development of our personality until we are finally able to experience the memory of the situation in which that particular hole formed.

We can look at each quality, see when it was lost, and what results. Sometimes combinations of qualities get lost. For instance, you might lose your strength, your will, and your love, and these would be a composite hole. So a whole psychological perspective can be built around the psychology of holes, which is the psychology of the personality, the false pearl.

S: I've noticed that lots of times when a man invalidates me, I'll feel a hole. I don't seem to be strong enough to stay with it before it fills up with panic and longing and self-devaluation, and soon I'm identifying with those feelings again. Would it be just a matter of practice to let myself feel the hole in a more direct way?

AH: Yes. That's what I'm saying. We work to tolerate those feelings, to stay with them and not try to fill the hole with something else. Sometimes the filling happens automatically. That is why the personality is called automatic. It is mechanical. After a while, everything happens automatically. You don't even know you're filling holes.

S: How do you slow down the process? By simply seeing it?

AH: Yes, by seeing it while you also have some awareness that you're trying to fill a hole. It is helpful to resist filling the hole. You might take an aim: "For the next two weeks, I will not try to get approval from the outside," or "Every time I see myself wanting to get approval from the outside, I will just observe this and not act on it." That's one way of doing it. Really, everything we're doing in the Work is to deal with these issues. Today we're looking at it from a particular perspective which can give you a certain understanding that can facilitate your work.

The actions of the personality are two-pronged. One prong is always attempting to avoid the hole, to avoid pain, and to experience pleasure. This is automatic. The other prong of the personality is always attempting to fill the hole as soon as something happens to expose it. This is also automatic. The false personality is mechanical in the sense that after you lose an essential quality and there is a hole, your personality automatically tries to fill it with false qualities from the outside.

Most of the time you are so identified with your attempt to fill holes that you don't think it's possible to not do this. So when you're feeling low, you get somebody to praise you. What else can you do? Really, that's what most people think. If you're feeling unlovable, find somebody who likes you. People usually identify with these patterns so completely that there is no chance of changing them.

To begin to work on such a pattern, first you need to observe it happening over and over, and see that it doesn't really work. Generally, people don't come here until they have begun to see that their way doesn't work. Most people believe in their strategy so completely that they think if they just get better at it and do it a few more years, it will work. Maybe they haven't found the right person or the right situation yet. If they just make a little more money, things will work out. It becomes apparent, to those who observe themselves, that these patterns don't get them what they really want. These are the people who come here. I don't mean that people who come to the Work have decided to experience their holes. No! When people first come here, they actually want to find better methods to fill their holes. That's why everybody comes. "I'll find a better way to get somebody to love me. I'll get better at my resolve to lose weight. I'll get ways to be this and that." So they come and they slowly find out that the Work is about something else.

It takes a long time for people to understand that trying to fill the hole doesn't work. Even as you're listening to me now, you're trying to fill holes through some understanding. "If I just know what the story is, then things should be better." What I'm saying is effective only if you're starting to *feel* your holes, which means you're starting to feel your emptiness. If you're filling it with words or ideas, you're just filling it again.

People try to fill holes in different ways. A woman may think, "Oh, so that's what I'm doing with my husband! I'm trying to use him to fill my holes. Okay, now I won't talk to him for the next two weeks." She is trying to fill her holes by blaming her husband for filling them in the past. It is very clever how we try to fill our holes. "Aha! Now I won't look for a new job; I won't try to make more money because that's just filling holes and he says it won't work to make more money." These thoughts will persist as you continue to try to fill some other hole.

I think this perspective gives us a particular perspective on society: The hole is taking over! Most of the time, society is attempting to fill holes. What do you think commercials are about? They appeal to your holes. They find a certain hole and try to give you the best filling for it. Good advertising agents are very effective with holes; they see which holes their product can fill, and they appeal to that hole. They make millions that way.

S: Does advertising appeal to existing holes, or does it create new ones?

AH: Your holes are created in your childhood. I don't think advertisers can actually create new holes. They emphasize the existing holes and appeal to them in different ways. Take the need to be beautiful, for instance. Some women feel they are not beautiful. You can appeal to this deficiency in many ways. Advertising stimulates and rein-forces the hole-filling mechanism. It stimulates the desires that result from the holes.

Inside your holes are pictures of what you think you want from the outside. Our unconscious is made of these images, and we keep looking for what's in those pictures. Adver-tising works at the level of the craving. It says, "If you buy this product, you'll be beautiful. If you buy that one, you'll be happy, or prosperous, or immortal."

S: Why couldn't advertising be used to stimulate your craving for Essence?

AH: Because they wouldn't make much money.

S: Wouldn't that be a powerful craving, the craving for Essence?

AH: It's the most powerful one. All religious systems and churches advertise that. They appeal on a deep level. Of course, very rarely can they actually lead people to Essence.

S: Is the desire to fill other people's holes just another way of filling your own?

AH: Yes. Sometimes you avoid your own holes by believ-ing other people have holes and you don't.

S: Or seeing other people as needy?

AH: Could be. There is a mechanism of avoiding your holes by projecting them outside. You say, "Other people are needy, and I'm going to help them." This process of filling holes is not superficial or simple; it is very deep and subtle and goes to the roots of your being. It requires very deep work to undo the process of the personality, reverse it, and return to Essence.

THREE

The Diamond Approach to the Work

We call the approach to the work we do here, the Diamond Approach. What do we mean by this? There are two levels of meaning. One of them is literal and the other metaphorical. The literal meaning is the more difficult to grasp because understanding it requires an experience of it, so for now I will talk only about the metaphorical meaning.

"Diamond Approach" means the method that uses the qualities of the diamond, what I call *diamond perception.* The diamond has an extraordinary precision and it can cut through hard materials without being destroyed. The approach we use here is focused and precise like laser surgery. Also, like the diamond, our approach is durable, valuable, and precious.

We also use the phrase "the Work" when talking about the Diamond Approach. It is helpful to know what this refers to so we can understand more exactly what we are doing here. As far as we know, human beings have always been different from animals in that people suffer a specific kind of pain that other creatures don't. All forms of life suffer sickness, accidents, death. But in addition to these, humans experience emotional and mental suffering and anguish. We know that throughout recorded history, human beings have experienced emotional pain, dissatisfaction, lack of contentment, and lack of peace. What people are experiencing now is nothing new; it has always existed. Maybe our suffering is greater than it was thousands of years ago, but it is still generally the same suffering.

In addition to this universal condition, there have always existed a few people with the knowledge that most of this suffering is due to man's alienation from himself. Most of our dissatisfaction comes not from sickness or material problems, but from not being ourselves. Not much can be done about the suffering caused by sickness or aging. Some people have seen, however, that emotional suffering is not inevitable in the same way. It is due to not knowing who we are, to not knowing Being, our true nature, not being free to be ourselves. It is this alienation which leaves us with a sense of emptiness and deep suffering that, in time, lead to physical difficulties, psychosomatic diseases, and other problems.

Along with this knowledge of the cause of our suffering, there has also existed the knowledge of how to lead a person back to himself, if he wants and is able to follow. "The Work" is any way, school, or method that recognizes the fact of suffering and the cause of unnecessary suffering and works to lead a person back to his true nature, which will eliminate the unnecessary suffering.

The purpose of the Work, however, is not primarily to eliminate suffering. The desire to return to one's true nature is an innate impulse that is there even in the absence of suffering. The more we are in touch with ourselves, the more we feel this innate desire to know and be who we really are. We want the freedom to live as we're supposed to live, to fulfill all our potential. When we don't live that way, we suffer. That suffering, rather than being a problem that the Work aims to solve, is simply a hunger for our true selves. It is a signal that we want to return to our true nature. The purpose of many schools and methods throughout history has been to bring people back to their true nature. This impulse has inspired religions and spiritual movements all over the world. The Work, we see, is very old. It has existed as long as humanity.

So what, more specifically, is the Diamond Approach to the Work? To come closer to an understanding of the Diamond Approach, we can look at the difficulty of the Work. It has always been assumed that it is very difficult to actually do the Work by those who are in the Work or who have established schools for the Work. It has also been assumed that very few people, only a small part of humanity, will attempt to take the path of returning, that fewer still will get anywhere, and that even fewer will actually complete the path. The path is perilous and, because of this, very few have attempted it, and very, very few have completed it. This is how it has been seen: that the nature of the Work itself is difficult and perilous. What we are now learning, however, is that, contrary to the assumptions of the past, it is not the nature of the Work to be so difficult. The reason it has seemed so up until now is primarily due to the fact that we have not had a certain kind of knowledge—what we call psychological knowledge.

It has been assumed, for instance, that a person needs tremendous will and determination to be able to do the Work. The task does require tremendous will and determination, and in the past, the failure to use sufficient will was blamed on the student. The teacher said that the student was not committed enough, not determined enough, didn't use his will enough. And this was true. It has always been and still is the case in the Work. So the teachers pushed the students, doing all kinds of things to get them through—tempting them, driving them—whatever might succeed in getting them to use their will and determination to continue working.

Now we understand that a person cannot use his will if the will is blocked or repressed. We know that the will gets blocked and repressed for specific reasons. Our work in this group has shown us that one of the many causes of this repression is the fear of feeling castrated. This unconscious fear is well known and documented in the psychoanalytic literature, though its connection with the will is generally not seen. The moment a person tries to use his will, he begins to experience a terrible fear, the fear of castration. It may be sexual castration or the castration of one's self, one's energy, one's will. The person doesn't even know this fear is there. He only knows that his will is not available, that he cannot act with determination, cannot do difficult things.

How is this person going to find his will if he feels something terrible is going to happen to him if he gets close to it? This fear can manifest as feeling that "something's going to happen to me," or "I'm going to die," or "I'm going to have an accident"—things like that. No matter how persuasive the teacher is, the person cannot get close to these fears. It's not that he doesn't want to use his will; it's that he doesn't know how to—he can't. Due to repression, his will is not available. It has been cut off because of specific unconscious fears. Because the fears are unconscious, the conscious mind has no control over them. So when you push against the fears, they get stronger. The teacher may then tell the student to "surrender." The student may know that surrender is the best thing but not know how to do this. The idea of surrendering brings terror. *What do you mean, surrender?* To the unconscious, surrender means loss, giving up part of oneself, disintegration, terrible things.

It has also been said that very few people do the Work because most people will not commit themselves sufficiently. People don't want to commit to the path because they're afraid of losing their personal freedom. The teacher then blames the student for not being committed enough. She says, "You should be more committed," or "You just don't know what's good for you."

This may well be true, but it doesn't solve anything. Students try to be committed, but we know now that the issue of commitment is related to some very deep difficulties. We know, for instance, that for a person to be able to really commit to the Work, she has to deal with her unconscious fears about separation. There is a deep fear in all of us of losing our sense of identity, our sense of who we are, our separateness, our individuality. Although there is no real loss of these things in the Work—quite the opposite in fact—there are genuine reasons for these fears. They come from unconscious beliefs that originated in infancy. The unconscious believes that if the person commits herself, she's going to lose herself. There is a sense in which this is true. When we do the Work, we go through a separation from the false personality with which we are identified in the beginning. To maintain a commitment to the Work, we must work through these fears of loss of identity. Only then is it possible to see and develop our true identity.

To commit to the Work so that you can find yourself does not make sense to most people because of their unconscious beliefs about commitment. "What do you mean, commit myself?" asks the unconscious. "If I commit myself, what will be left of me?" We know from our Work how acute and compelling these anxieties are. We recognize that many of these anxieties are unconscious; at first we don't even know they exist. They just influence us. We can see this in relationships. We know how hard it is to commit ourselves in relationships even when we feel that we have found the person we've been looking for and our troubles should now be over. The unconscious says, "Wait a minute! What's going to happen to me now?" These same unconscious conflicts surface when you want to commit yourself to the Work. So we see that it has been difficult to do the Work because the commitment, the will, the understanding are generally not available due to repressed fears and resistances that are completely unconscious, that control our behavior, and that get stronger if we push against them.

Since the false personality is the barrier that blocks our contact with our true nature, the Work has always required that people begin to make changes in patterns of behavior that are manifestations of the false personality. To help students disidentify with the personality, Work schools have taught people not to be selfish but to be generous and compassionate. Yet telling students not to be selfish is dealing with the personality in a way that we now know doesn't work very well. For example, we have certain fears and deficiencies that make us greedy; we are not going to stop being greedy simply because someone tells us to. Perhaps we unconsciously believe we must struggle to get enough just to survive, even when this is clearly not true in our actual circumstances. Whether we consciously believe this or not, we will feel greedy as long as the unconscious belief is there.

The unconscious fears and tensions that act as barriers to the experience of Essence and to the flow of physical and subtle energies are seen through the subtle senses as a certain kind of darkness, a block in the energy flow. Many techniques have been developed through the years to get around these barriers, these dark spots, and let the energy move. Some use exercises or postures to get around certain barriers.

Some push through the dark spots by sheer force of will or dedication: ten hours a day of meditation for ten years, things like that. These methods are very powerful, and they work—but usually only for the lucky person who doesn't have many barriers or such strong ones to begin with.

Those in the Work have known that these barriers have to do with conditioning and that the false personality arises from conditioning. A lot has been known about the qualities of the false personality, how it behaves, how it moves away from Essence. Some methods have worked on developing "antidotes" for each dark quality; these may take the form of different meditations, exercises, visualizations, yoga postures, and so on. In these methods, the teachers have had to work intensely to push and pull students through barriers, usually with limited success.

Because of the difficulty of the path, students have generally been accepted into the Work (especially in serious schools) only if they are desperate enough to lay their lives on the line for it. The teachers have known that unless a student is willing to do this, the path can never be completed. It is simply too difficult because of the fears and resistance involved. There have been all kinds of selection procedures; a person can be tested for years before he is accepted into the Work. This has been necessary (and is still the practice in most serious schools) because it is a waste of time for a teacher to spend time with a student who will not progress on the path.

So we see that very few people have been able to do the Work, to learn what Essence is and know the fullness of what it is to be a true human being, an adult of the species rather than a baby. Most people are only a few years old in terms of their essential development. Very few adults exist.

It is the developments in psychology that have occurred primarily in the twentieth century that allow us to see how people are stuck in, and controlled by, their childhood conditioning. The approach of psychology and psycho-therapy, which has arisen in the West, is a new approach to the problem of emotional suffering. Since the time of Freud, much knowledge has accumulated about the unconscious and the personality. Psychology, the science of the mind, provides a lot of understanding that has been lacking in the Work. But those who developed the knowledge and practice of psychology are not, in general, those who are in the Work. They work to alleviate suffering by trying to resolve conflicts on an emotional level. As a rule, Essence is not recognized in psychology and psychotherapy, so the alienation from Essence is not seen. It is seen that people are not in touch with their emotions and their sensations; it is seen that people are controlled by complex structures of unconscious beliefs, fears, and defenses. But that extra dimension, the existence of the true being, is not generally seen or taken into consideration in psychological theory.

Psychological theories and therapeutic approaches are proliferating these days, but none of them seems complete, and they have different rates of success. From the perspective of the Work, it is clear that these approaches cannot be completely successful in eliminating suffering if they don't take into consideration the fact of Essence and of our alienation from it. The most basic cause of our suffering is not emotional conflict. We have emotional conflict because we don't know our true nature. This is different from the view of psychology which sees emotional conflicts as the cause of suffering. Problems in childhood with the environment create conflicts in our unconscious minds which, in turn, cause difficulties in our day-to-day life. What is not seen is that these conflicts create alienation from the essential parts of ourselves that are the source of our happiness, joy, and fulfillment.

Suppose that whenever a man expressed his anger as a child, his mother rejected him, withdrew, or was frightened.

Since the mother is identified with love and merging (at least in infancy and early childhood), when this man later experiences anger, he will fear the loss of love and merging. In his past, the qualities of love and merging were not compatible with anger. His mother withdrew her love when he expressed it. In this Work, we understand that strength and sexuality are closely related to anger; they both involve the energy of separation or aggression. So when this man experiences love and merging with another person or situation, he will feel a threat to his strength and sexuality. This is the fabric of pain and confusion we suffer in our daily lives. As many of you have seen in your work here, we generally cannot approach the essential states connected with love, anger, or sex without experiencing anxiety, fear, even panic.

So what does this mean? Our childhood experiences of frustration, conflict, and rejection result in the loss of essential states. Since it is these qualities for which we long, the confusion and discontent in our adult lives is bound to be rooted in this loss. The loss is experienced as a feeling of emptiness, meaninglessness, deadness, deficiency.

To summarize, we see that the effectiveness of Work schools has been limited by a lack of knowledge of the specific unconscious barriers that prevent us from experiencing the corresponding essential states that make up our true nature. The effectiveness of psychotherapy has been limited by its ignorance of essential states; resolutions occur on the levels of ego and emotions, which are not the levels on which we are ultimately satisfied.

In the past decade, some people have begun to integrate these two approaches and have had some degree of success, depending on their experience and knowledge. This is not yet the Diamond Approach to the Work. So far, the attempts at integrating the Work with the knowledge of conditioning and the structure of the unconscious has been very general. It has been effective for some people, but it still perpetuates an unnecessary split between the student, who is still largely identified with his false personality, and that student's experience of Essence. So far, the pattern is that the psychological work is expected to take students from point A to point B. Then the Work takes them from point B to point C. Psychological work is undertaken to dissolve the false personality; it is only then that the possibility for essential development exists.

The Diamond Approach is different from these approaches in that it works on the perception and dissolution of the false personality simultaneously with the perception and development of essential states. To explain how this method works, I will summarize what we call the Theory of Holes.

In the history and literature of the Work, we see that knowledge of what we are calling "Essence" is the goal of the Work. In Western philosophy, we find Plato talking about pure ideas, or the Platonic forms. Plato, a student of Socrates (who was doing the Work), wrote about Socrates' discussions with his students concerning what are called the "eternal verities." (We call them the qualities of Essence. These include courage, truth, humility, love, and so on.) Socrates wanted to show how people learn these things. He demonstrated that we can't learn these from someone else. No one can teach you the quality of courage or love. In his final arguments, he showed that we know these things only by remembering them.

Everyone has some memory of these essential forms. We have seen in our work that a consistent characteristic of essential states is the feeling that you have known it before, you have been here before, you are recalling a more fundamental reality that, in the process of living, you had forgotten. So we know that although we are generally unaware of it, this memory of Essence exists, and we know that the process of remembering our Essence is the process of remembering ourselves, of returning to our true nature.

Another thing we need to know in order to understand how our method works is that Essence is not one big lump, not one state or experience or mode of being. Essence has (or is) many states or qualities. There is truth; there is love; there is compassion; there is objective consciousness; there is value; there is will; there is strength; there is joy. All these are different qualities of Essence. They are different facets of the diamond, reflecting different colors.

Although it has always been known that Essence has many facets, most schools have emphasized one quality or cluster of qualities more than others. Some schools, for instance, emphasize Love. They use techniques to develop Love. They talk about Love. They pray. They chant. They worship the guru. They worship God. They surrender to Love. Other approaches emphasize service and work. They use the belly centers more. Others emphasize Truth or the search for Truth. Others—Gurdjieff, for example—emphasized Will, making supreme efforts. Whichever aspects of Essence are emphasized by a given method depends on the experience and character of the teacher or the originator of the method. Often a teacher will have had to work through a certain part of himself more deeply than other parts. The quality of Essence associated with that part may be very strong. Since it is through that quality that the teacher reached the understanding and embodiment of Essence, he develops his method of teaching around that quality.

Very few schools have worked with the totality of Essence. This leads to an apparent discord between the different teachings. Mohammed speaks very differently from Jesus, and the Buddha tells it his way. Present teachers say different things. Some say surrender to God. Some look for the "blue pearl." Some say to make a conscious effort, to look for your will. Some say the answer is the Void. Since most of these people don't know that Essence has many qualities, each thinks the others are wrong. If you believe that great efforts of will are leading you to your essence, it will seem obvious to you that love will not work. Love may imply weakness, sentimentality. So in some groups, at least for a time, the will is developed at the cost of love because they appear incompatible.

We know that Essence is something we learn about by remembering it—recalling what we once knew. You have all had direct experience of this. So when and why did we forget that which we are now working to remember?

Everyone is born with Essence. Just as as your physical body follows a certain pattern of growth, so does your essence. The newborn baby is mainly in the state we call "the essence of the Essence," a nondifferentiated state of unity. At about three months, the baby is in a "merged" state which is necessary for the development of the relationship with the mother. After the merged state, Strength develops, then Value, Joy, the Personal Essence, and so on. But because of interference from, and conflict with, the environment, this development is only partial. Every time there is pain or trauma, there is a lessening of a certain quality of Essence. Which quality is affected depends on the nature and the time of the trauma. Sometimes our strength, sometimes our love, sometimes our self-valuing, compassion, joy, or intuition is hurt and eventually blocked.

When a quality of Essence is blocked from a person's experience, what is left in place of that quality is a sense of emptiness, a deficiency, a hole, as we saw in our discussion of the Theory of Holes. You have seen in your work here how you actually experience that emptiness as a hole in your body where a quality of Essence is cut off. This creates the sense that something is lacking and, therefore, something is wrong. When we feel a deficiency, we try to fill the hole. Since Essence has been cut off in that place, we cannot fill the hole with Essence, so we try to fill it with similar, false qualities, or we try to fill it from the outside.

Suppose, for instance, that our love for our mother is rejected, not valued. That love in us is hurt, wounded. To avoid experiencing the hurt, we deaden a certain part of our body, and in that way we are cut off from the sweet quality of love in ourselves. Where that love should be, we have an emptiness, a hole. Forgetting that it was *our* love that was lost, we think that we lost something from outside and try to get it back from outside. We want someone to love us, so the hole will be filled with love.

Connected with the hole are the memories of the situations that brought the hurt and also the memory of what was lost. It is all there, but repressed. Since we do not consciously remember what happened or what we lost, we are left with the sense of emptiness and the false qualities or ideas we are trying to fill the hole with. In time, these holes accumulate. They are filled by various emotions and beliefs, and this material becomes the content of our identity, our personality. We think we are those things. Some people are left with a bit of Essence here and there, but in those whose childhood problems were most severe, everything is repressed, resulting in a subjective sense and look of dullness, almost deadness.

It is the knowledge of these processes that makes the work we do here, the Diamond Approach, possible. Now we are able to be very clear, very precise. We have an obvious way to lead people back to themselves. First, people must learn to sense themselves, to pay attention to themselves, so that the necessary information is available. Most people go through life without this self-awareness because they are trying to avoid feeling the emptiness, the falseness, the something-is-wrong feeling. You can't avoid self-awareness and do this Work.

The things that can empower your work include whatever will you've got and whatever love for yourself and understanding you have. You must have some openness (conscious or not) to your desire to return to your true nature. In addition, you must have some understanding that your difficulties come from inside you. If you fundamentally believe that your problems will be solved by making more money, becoming more beautiful, having children, getting a better car, and so on, you cannot do the Work. The Work begins by seeing that the difficulties come from inside us and sensing that the fulfillment we seek will also come from inside.

Next, we use various forms of the old techniques, such as meditations, to strengthen different parts of Essence. We also use various psychological techniques to understand the blocks against the issues around the different aspects of Essence. You can observe in yourself certain clusters of behaviors that surround a given issue at any particular time in your life. If you continue to work on these, you will observe that you're behaving in these ways to fill a certain deficiency or hole.

In this Work, we see how different qualities of Essence are related to specific issues from the past. The relationships between the essential state, the hole that resulted from the loss of that state, the emotions and beliefs we create to fill the holes, and the conflicts that arise from the resulting false personality are all understood. These relationships and patterns are the same for every human being. When a person is working here in the group, I can tell by what issue he is working on which essential state and which deficiency are involved.

For instance, the loss of the Will is generally related to fears about castration as we discussed earlier. The loss of Strength is related to repression of anger and also fear of separation from mother. The loss of Compassion is always due to the suppression of hurt. Each hole is generally filled by the same thing, with variations depending on childhood history and the cultural and social circumstances of the person. Compassion, for instance, might be replaced by sentimentality and belief that one is a loving person. Intuition might be replaced by excessive ideation, and Strength by a show of being tough.

If you deal thoroughly with the set of issues related to a given state, if you see the aspect of the false personality that attempted to fill the hole, and if you go all the way into that sense of emptiness, you will get to the quality that has been lost. We have seen this over and over again in our work here.

Psychotherapists deal with the issues, but in general, they go back only as far as the deficiency. They see the original issues and work at resolving them. They don't see that the emptiness comes from a lack of Essence. They see only the sense of emptiness and the conflicts that result from the childhood history. I'm sure that clients in therapy sometimes get to essential states, but the usual therapist doesn't see it, and the client herself won't perceive it as significant. She will only know that she feels wonderful, relieved, and will sometimes even have a strong sense of having "come home to herself." Unfortunately, the essential state will not be recognized for what it is; the experience will be ignored by the therapist and lost by the client, never pursued or developed.

When you work with a person who knows that it is possible to go through the experience of loss all the way back to that which was lost and who recognizes these essential qualities, then it becomes possible to see and develop your true nature. In this Work, we are not interested in just going back through your childhood to understand your conditioning and your conflicts. We go back to the original hole and simply experience it without trying to fill it.

In therapy, if you deal with the conflict that you wanted your father who was emotionally unavailable to you, you feel deep hurt. You see that you can't get your father in the present, so the resolution is to relate to another man (sometimes the therapist himself) to fill those holes. This resolution doesn't work. You can try to fill the deficiency of the loss of love with the love of another man, but since it is your own love, your own will, for which you ultimately long, you will feel dissatisfied with the love and support from the father substitute, whomever it is you are using to fill the deficiency.

In this Work, we know that you can experience your love or will only by allowing yourself to experience the holes and deficiencies associated with them. This is difficult and frightening. A lot of spiritual disciplines use techniques to enable students to stay with these things. When you can finally do that, then the real resolution can happen, the resolution not of simply resolving the emotional conflict but of retrieving the lost quality. It is the presence of the quality of love that will eliminate the problem of love for you, and the presence of will that will eliminate the sense of castration or powerlessness. Nothing else will do.

You have seen that you can begin with any emotions, thoughts, or difficulties and work through them, right to the original deficiency. By staying with this process, following each issue all the way, you will finally have the memory of what you lost, as Socrates said. And by remembering it, you will have it. Everything you have lost you can regain by working like this. Everything.

We understand that there is no separation between psychological issues and Essence; they are intertwined, woven together. This is why you cannot set to work to eliminate the false personality and, when that's done, start experiencing and developing Essence. Without the retrieval of that which the personality was created to replace, personality simply cannot be dissolved.

The reason the Diamond Approach can be precise is that we know that each aspect of Essence is connected with certain psychological conflicts. We can use powerful psychological techniques to help us perceive and understand these conflicts, repressions, and patterns of resistance. We don't need to push against the resistances, the dark spots; we simply shed light on them. After a while, they disintegrate. Then the passage is easy. We can flow through those places rather than have to go around them. Going around them or pushing through them is the hard way, the long way. Our way has more to do with understanding, with the precise diamond clarity.

We can take this understanding and see it in relation to other psychological approaches and Work schools. Just as different Work schools emphasize different aspects of Essence, various psychological approaches emphasize different deficiencies or holes. Each school of psychology was developed by a person working on or through the dominant deficiencies that they perceived. Take Freud, for instance. What did he emphasize? First he perceived the existence of the unconscious. He saw the repressed material of the unconscious as consisting mostly of the aggressive force and the sexual libido. The aggressive force is what we call the Strength essence, and the libido is a combination of two aspects of Essence, the Strength and the Merging Love. Freud was dealing with the issues around deficiencies in these qualities. He saw the barrier of castration anxiety which, as we have discussed, produces a loss of Will. Freudian psychology is very effective with these deficiencies. It can go all the way through to the essential qualities associated with them.

Reich was basically dealing with the quality of Pleasure and the deficiency that has to do with the loss of Pleasure, especially sexual pleasure. Reichian techniques are oriented toward showing a person the ways in which he's not in touch with his body, showing him that he cannot tolerate Pleasure. Reichian work is designed to go into and through the barriers to Pleasure.

What did Fritz Perls emphasize? To learn to be in the here and now with no explanation, no past. A clue to which hole Perls' approach dealt with is the fact that he went to Japan to study with a Zen master. Why was he interested in Zen? Because the quality the Zen Buddhists deal with is the essence of completeness—that to be completely here and now is to see the true nature of things. This is what we call the aspect of Brilliancy, and what Zen people call the *Buddha nature*. Zen Buddhists are not concerned with dealing with any of the specific qualities; they want to go straight through to the end. Now Perls knew this intuitively, although he didn't quite know what he was looking for. He must have had some of this quality of Brilliancy pulling him toward Zen and eventually toward his development of Gestalt Therapy, which has the same goal. But Zen was too hard, too slow. Only one in ten thousand students makes it through the Zen approach, and then only after sitting and staring at a wall ten hours a day for years. No excitement, nothing. If you can tolerate sitting for maybe twenty years and let all the resistances move through you, you might end up seeing the nature of the wall. Because it was this quality that was strongest in Perls, he developed his continuum of awareness and the various Gestalt techniques that have proven so powerful in helping people penetrate or make transparent the workings of their false personalities.

The neo-Freudians, the ego psychologists, deal mainly with the deficiency of Value and self-esteem, the deficiencies of the various flavors of Love that come from object relationships, and the deficiency that results from the absence of the Personal Essence, which is true individuality. Their knowledge is amazingly specific in terms of how these holes develop, although they don't know about the essential qualities themselves because they work mainly on an ego level. Their knowledge, however, is very useful. We've been using it here to great advantage when people are learning about their Personal Essence, their value, and their ability to experience actual love for another person.

In the Diamond Approach, we use these various techniques to find out exactly what emotional conflicts contributed to the loss of a particular quality of Essence. We then go right into the emptiness itself. This makes it possible to remember the aspect that was lost. It never fails. For example, we have seen time and again in our work that everyone who deals with her attachment to her mother and goes all the way into the feelings of need, longing, and hurt will ultimately get into what we call the Merging quality of Essence. It's a wonderful merging kind of love where you lose your boundaries and merge with everything.

So you see that although we accomplish the tasks of psychotherapy in the course of doing this Work, our interest is not in psychotherapy. Our interest is in the Work. Without actually doing the work on Essence, there is no resolution to our suffering and no opportunity to realize our true nature.

There is no need for us to work only on problems and symptoms here, and there is no need to isolate ourselves in a monastery in order to work on Essence. In fact, we need to do this work while we are in the world. It is while we are in relationships, while we're working at our jobs, having trouble with our cars, dealing with money problems, that we have the material we need to work with. Using the psychological techniques along with Work methods allows us to accomplish the aim of the Work in an easier, more efficient way than has often been possible in the past.

It is necessary to see that our search for understanding and truth are the most important things, for these things will eventually lead to the possibility of experiencing and developing all aspects of our Essence. It doesn't work to try to develop one aspect of Essence without the others.

We're not trying, for instance, to develop love alone. We don't want you to just be loving. If you have love but you have no will, your love will not be real. Or if you have will but no love, you will be powerful and strong, but without any idea of real humanity, enjoyment, or love. If you have love and will but no objective consciousness, then your love and your will may be directed toward the wrong things. Your actions will not be exact or appropriate. Only the development of all the qualities will enable us to become true, full human beings.

The Work we do here requires commitment, dedication, and sincerity. We don't require these things absolutely, because we understand that there are barriers to them which must be worked through. Similarly, I don't ask for absolute obedience or absolute trust. I just ask you to try to understand yourself. Through your own experience, you will discover whether our approach is trustworthy or not, and in time you will see your barriers to trust. There is no need for blind trust, or blind love, or blind anything. The Diamond Approach is *seeing*; it is understanding.

In the beginning, the student needs only sincerity and the understanding that the barriers to fulfillment and the fulfillment itself are both inside. This is true for teachers as well. Additionally, the teacher must have the ability to embody the essential qualities and therefore to be able to perceive them in the student. It is required that I perceive your Essence and know what I am seeing. The only way I can know this is by tasting it, experiencing it within myself.

These are the same things that have always been required in the Work. Now we have added the new knowledge of this century, the tremendous knowledge of psychology. I think we're putting it to good use, using it the way it was meant to be used. I feel grateful to the people who developed this knowledge. Are there any questions?

S: I have a question about resistance. The Diamond Approach is to cut through resistance. How is it different from pushing? Is it like seeing through?

AH: Yes. Cutting through means seeing, understanding. It doesn't mean using scissors. It is diamond perception, the clear, precise perception, that cuts through. The clear, focused diamond perception will help you see exactly what the issues in your life are. By seeing and understanding them, the issues will then fall away automatically as you see what is true and what is false.

S: So it's not like there's resistance, and I'm pushing against it.

AH: No. Part of understanding is understanding the resistance to understanding. Part of the Work is to learn how to disidentify, to not believe your resistances and not identify with your emotional conflicts, but to see that they are a symptom of what is more fundamentally wrong. People take their deficiencies, their holes, as something wrong with them. Because they believe that something is wrong and nothing can be done about it, they're always trying to fill the hole. What else can they do? But we see here that the hole, the deficiency, the sense of need, is not the problem. What is wrong is a loss of a certain aspect of Essence.

We can take the knowledge that was arduously developed by Freud and his followers and use it for our Work. We will also continue to use certain of the old techniques: meditations and ways of paying attention to ourselves. And we have this very effective *Diamond knowledge* to remove the barriers with no detours, no going around, but going straight through to direct and complete understanding of ourselves.

You have to see through all your conflicts, your fears, your guilt, your anger, your love, everything, so that in time, more and more essential qualities will be realized in you. If you can do this work thoroughly and completely, in time you will be complete. No holes, just solid Essence. The Diamond Approach is following the threads from the suffering in our lives all the way back to Essence.

FOUR

Faith and Commitment

Student: Would you say something about faith?
AH: Faith is a word I seldom use. I think the best way to understand faith is to contrast it with belief. Faith, in a sense, does what belief attempts to do. That is why many people take faith to be belief. For instance, when people go to church, they are told to have faith. Most people think that means they have to believe in God and Christ and the doctrines of the church. So in the beginning, faith is seen as belief. "I believe there is a God, so I have faith in God. I believe that Christ died to save humanity and reduce our suffering. I believe this because somebody I trust told me." So faith, in its crudest form, is a belief or an outcome of a belief, a feeling you have because you believe something.

This is not real faith. Real faith results not from belief but from real knowledge. When you really know because you have perceived directly, then you have real faith. So real faith means the direct knowing of that which you have faith in. When you have perceived God, then you have real faith. It's unshakable because you have seen it, felt it. You may not be seeing it right now, but you have seen it at least once. So faith is belief in the existence of something that you have experienced or perceived directly. So you have the feeling or the emotion of faith.

There is belief; there is faith that results from belief; there is faith that results from knowledge; and there is knowledge. When knowledge is there all the time, there is no need for faith. I don't need to have faith in my Essence; I always know it's there. Most people take faith to mean the belief itself or the feeling that comes out of believing something—which means they still don't know. They will say, "I don't know. I just have faith that this is true." But when one knows, the faith is unshakable. When you know all the time, faith is gone. So in the beginning there is no faith, then there is faith, and at the end there is no faith. Faith is the intermediate state, the transition between belief and knowing.

In many religions, faith is important because the church leaders do not have precise, direct knowledge. They emphasize belief and devotion to the doctrine, although at the heart or beginning of most religions, there was actual knowledge, the direct experience. In some religions like Buddhism, you don't hear much about faith at all. They speak of it once in a while, but it's not a big deal. They rely more on the immediate, direct experience of something. At least that is what is emphasized in Buddhist texts.

S: So could faith be called trust in knowledge?

AH: That could be another meaning of faith. If you have the knowledge and you have faith in it, it means you trust it. But that is not complete knowledge yet. If you really know Essence and what it does, there is no need to trust it. Trust falls short of the complete, direct perception of knowledge. If I trust that something is going to come true, for example, I don't completely *know* it's going to come true. It is not direct knowledge yet.

S: I feel that even when you do know, trust and faith still exist.

AH: They increase. Both your trust in Essence and your faith increase, but after a while it's not a question of trust or faith. You just *know* as a direct, common-sense fact. There is no need to trust. You know that if you light the fire, it will be warm. Do you say you have faith that it will be warm? Do you need to trust that the fire is going to be warm?

S: I don't need to, but I could.

AH: Yes, but usually you don't say that you trust the fire is going to be warm. Because you know the fire is going to be warm. There is no doubt in your mind. That's why faith is contrasted with doubt. If I have faith, it means I don't have doubt. When I say the fire is hot, I do not mean I have faith that it will be hot—that is not the basic quality of my experience. The basic quality is that I know it.

Faith is seen more on the emotional level than as something that has to do with knowledge. It has to do with devotion or trust. Most people who consider themselves to be religious depend on faith. This isn't really any better than belief. Belief is mental faith, and faith is the emotional complement to belief.

When you have knowledge instead of belief at the mental level, what will the corresponding state at the heart level be? That's what is called "certainty." The certainty comes from the direct presence of what you know. The heart perceives Essence. The Essence is there, and the heart is tasting it. Essentially that is what the heart's function is in meditation. It has a tongue. Each person's heart can taste Essence.

I'm not saying that faith is not useful. It's very useful. The closer the beliefs are to the actual reality, the more useful they are. If what you believe in happens to actually be true—although you don't know it—then your belief can lead you to the truth. Faith can be used in a good way.

S: What is commitment?

AH: At its first level, commitment is what everybody takes it to be—the attitude of dedication. To say that I'm committed to doing something means that I'm dedicated to doing it: I've decided to marshal my will and all my forces to do it and to continue doing it. That's the usual meaning of commitment. Does anybody have a different idea about commitment?

S: I feel committed when I really like what I'm doing.

AH: Yes, so for you the motivation for commitment is to like something. If there's pleasure in it, then you can commit yourself.

Commitment is also connected with belief and faith. If you believe in something, you have faith in it, and you tend to commit yourself. The more you have faith in it, the more you tend to commit yourself. If you have faith in the Virgin Mary, you might commit yourself to going to church more often. You might commit yourself to saying your prayers morning and evening, putting your effort and your will into remembering to say them.

At the beginning, commitment depends on belief and on faith. But just as faith can be based on direct perception, so can commitment be based on direct perception. So there are gradations in commitment or in strength of commitment; there is belief, faith, and knowledge. If you have no belief in something, you have no commitment. If you have strong faith in something, you have a lot of commitment. If you know something, then you have even more commitment.

If you have complete knowledge of something, then you have complete commitment. What does it mean to have complete commitment?

S: When I feel really committed to something, it seems like part of me.

AH: Yes. Commitment, in this case, is the lack of separation from what you want. The more you're committed to something, the closer you are to it, and the less you separate yourself from it. When there's complete knowledge and complete commitment, there's complete union with what you want. Then you become it; you *are* that. So commitment becomes the embodiment of what you are committed to.

S: So then the act of will is not involved any more?

AH: That's right. The will is needed to get to that state of total commitment. At the beginning, you need to commit yourself a lot. When there's belief or some intuition that gives you faith, you can commit yourself; yet you need will and strength to continue. When you know more, you still need your will, but only because there are still barriers. The barriers are there because the knowledge is not complete. When the knowledge is complete, there are no barriers and no need for will. You don't need to *will* your essence to be there; it's just there.

Commitment is essentially dedication, bringing yourself closer to what you want to do. You use will to push yourself closer to what you want, to your aim. We say that at the essential level there is no such thing as faith; there is only knowledge. It is the same thing with commitment: In Essence, there is no such thing as commitment. There's just being. When you are your essence, you are not committed to yourself; you *are* yourself.

S: Could you connect this with what you said about holes? It seems that faith has something to do with really going all the way into a hole. I'll get a little way into a hole, and then I'll get terrified. It's as if I don't have the faith to go any further.

AH: Yes. You don't have faith at that time because you don't know what's really down there. You can go just so far trusting that you'll be okay. When it gets really scary, your faith starts getting shaky because your faith is still not the faith of direct perception. Despite this, sometimes you manage to keep going through the fear. You take what is called a "leap of faith." You leap and find out what is there. There might be snakes in the hole or something you've been searching for. You don't know. That's the leap of faith.

So faith can take you to a certain level, but it can't take you all the way. At some point, you have to take the leap from faith to knowledge. There is always a leap between mind and Essence. The mind of the personality can go just so far towards Essence; it can't go all the way. Essence and this quality of mind are in two different places, two different levels. You might go to the limit of the mind or to the limit of the emotions. That limit is still not Essence. You have to leap.

When you are at the limit of your faith, you see this huge, dark abyss. You might be able to say, "I'm going to jump." If there is somebody there you trust, that helps a lot. When somebody is there who will say, "Yes, I know what's inside that hole. I've been there. I'll hold your hand," you can reply, "All right. I'm scared as hell, but you say you've been there and you've come out of it, and you look pretty good, so I'll try it." Usually you can take that leap of faith by yourself only when you have to, when you have put yourself in circumstances that leave no choice. What else can you do? You can't go backward. It's true that you don't know what will happen, but you're tired of the same old business. You have to try something new. That something new is to jump into the abyss. One of the main functions of the teacher or the guide is to help you make that leap. When you are experiencing a certain hole, your guide might know that at the bottom of that abyss is a profound state or quality of Essence. Actually, the guide will most often be manifesting the quality beneath the abyss, which gives you more faith.

S: You were saying that sometimes a person will take a leap, a quantum leap, because nothing is left. None of the other things have worked. I see that you get to that point sometimes not because you've brought yourself there, but because people don't buy into your defenses. When a teacher doesn't support your defenses and that helps push you to the limit where you have to make that leap, isn't she using a kind of compassion?

AH: Yes. If you are with somebody who is guiding you and you come to an abyss and it's a matter of jumping or not jumping into the abyss, you will tend to leap if the guide is compassionate. If the compassion is not there, it will be very hard for you. So, when the teacher has compassion, it helps you to take the leap. You know the teacher doesn't want to hurt you, that she wants what is best for you, and that she isn't trying to trick you. If you doubt the teacher, it will be much more difficult for you to take the leap.

S: I have a question about commitment. You said that faith and belief are emotional and intellectual. Does commitment come from the belly, from instinct?

AH: Yes, that's a good point. Certainly the ultimate form of commitment is to *be*, and being does have to do with the belly. And we've also seen that commitment has to do with will. So, yes, commitment is essentially bringing your belly closer to something; it has to do with action, too.

S: Yesterday we talked about instincts, the instinct of self-preservation, and how the instincts are pure energy. That's what it feels like commitment is—pure energy, the instinct for survival.

AH: That's true. In a sense, everybody always has a very powerful, strong commitment. But the issue here is what

they are committing to. How we use the energy of the instincts depends on whether the energy is free or distorted.
If it is distorted, then a person will commit himself to something that is not essential. If your sexual instinct is distorted, you're basically committed to your boyfriend's penis.
If your self-preservation instinct is distorted, you might be
committed to money. Many people are committed to making money. You hear stories of someone who starts with
nothing and ends up being a millionaire; that takes tremendous commitment. Obviously, the self-preservation instinct
is there, but it is directed toward an aim that does not have
to do with the truth of the instinct.

S: I didn't understand completely what you said about
the survival instinct and going after money.

AH: Everyone has a survival instinct. Our most powerful instinct is for the survival of the organism. Now, survival is basically simple: It involves having shelter and
enough food and taking care of yourself. But if a person's
instinct for survival is distorted because of certain childhood experiences, he might become fearful that he won't
be able to provide enough for himself. He feels insecure
because of something that happened in his childhood that
interfered with and blocked the energy. Perhaps his parents died, or expected him to take care of himself before
he was actually emotionally or physically able to do so.

If the person is basically insecure about survival, then
he will need a great many things to fill that hole in order
to feel secure. A person who isn't insecure might feel fine
making a thousand dollars a month, but a person who feels
a deep insecurity won't feel secure if he makes just an ade-
quate income that covers his needs. He will keep thinking
he should make more. One thousand dollars a month this
year may be all right, but next year he will want to earn
two thousand a month—even if he doesn't spend it. The
insecurity doesn't go away.

Insecurity has nothing to do with how much you've got; it has to do with a basic feeling in your unconscious. And it will not go away when you try to get security from outside. Security issues can revolve around various things— money, power, friends. Whenever the self-preservation instinct is blocked and the energy is not flowing, there is a basic sense of insecurity. People are usually very identified with their feelings of insecurity and will do almost anything to try to fill that hole rather than simply feel it. They are unaware of a blockage in a certain part of their body. Thus, the feeling can't be addressed.

It's revealing that certain kinds of financial holdings are called "securities." People may buy them to fill the hole of insecurity. Someone might have millions of dollars in securities and still need more, or have dozens of friends and still need more, or have lots of power and still need more. There's an interesting thing that can happen here. If the person has the hole of insecurity, then the more he's got in securities, the more he tends to feel the absence of security—which is the hole—and the more he will feel compelled to acquire more securities. He would rarely say, "Now I have enough money." It seems that the satisfaction of the mistaken desires allows the dissatisfaction connected with the hole to surface. This explains how having more money can make someone more insecure. Howard Hughes was completely financially secure, but I wouldn't be surprised if his basic motivation for making money was insecurity. The more money he made, the more paranoid and insecure he became.

S: I have a question about knowledge. If we had absolute knowledge, we would have an absolute state of freedom from false personality and superego. Yet sometimes we experience moments of absolute knowledge followed by denial. You see your state, and then you say it's your imagination or just an experience because there's no total knowledge to reinforce the partial knowledge. How do you differentiate at such times between what is experiential truth and what is just imagination?

AH: For you, that is very easy. Whenever you see something, just ask yourself, "Is this true?" Look, and truth arises. Since you know what truth is, you can do that. Isn't that simple? But before someone can recognize the truth, he or she needs to do all kinds of work. Everything you do here is to become clearer and clearer, until you are certain about what you experience. To do that, you must go through all the lies.

When I talk about absolute knowledge, I don't mean you will always feel you have absolute knowledge. But when you experience Essence and you are your essence, then you are your true self, and there is absolute knowledge about what you are being. The knowledge and the being are the same thing. That is absolute knowledge. It is not total knowledge because there are other things about Essence you are not experiencing at that time. When you experience your value, for instance, you have absolute knowledge of your value. But you don't have absolute knowledge about truth at that moment unless you become the part of Essence that has everything—the all-knowing, omniscient part. When you are experiencing that all-knowing part, then you can experience that you have total knowledge.

S: I experienced that all-knowing part in a session. At the time, I knew that I knew. Later, I wondered what exactly it was that I knew that I knew.

AH: That is a very important observation. It reveals the crucial distinction between Essence and the mind. Essential knowing is the same as Essence because *knowing Essence is being Essence.* It is direct perception, direct embodiment of Essence. When Essence is not there, you try to remember it. However, the mind cannot reach Essence; it will try to remember Essence, but it cannot. Our normal, mental memory can't remember the state of Essence. There is no way for the mind to do it.

You experienced an aspect of Essence a few days ago. You remember it, but not exactly. You can't remember the most important element. It's not there. When the Essence is not there, there is no knowledge. The mind is there, and the experience of the mind usually is dulled by skepticism. It's very good at doubting. You see, the mind does not have certainty about Essence. It cannot. Essence is beyond mind. Essence is not within the realm of mind. Mind only has images of Essence, perceptions of it.

S: It's like living in a world within a world. There are two separate levels, two separate awarenesses. One is knowing, and the other is thinking about knowing.

AH: Yes. The knowledge of the mind is not the most real knowledge. The most real knowledge is the substance, the honey that the Sarmoun Darq collect. The content of the mind is information. Information can be *about* real knowledge, but it is not knowledge yet. Information contains memories, theories, descriptions, images, but real knowledge is taste. What you taste, you know. If you do not taste, you do not know. But that doesn't mean that if you tasted it before, you know it now. Yet if you can remember that you knew, and remember exactly what you knew, if you can remember it totally, Essence will no longer be a memory; it will be there now. So memory can help us get back to real knowledge. Memory can reach toward it and come very close. Then we must leap, and the essential knowledge will be there.

FIVE

Nobility and Suffering

S tudent: In one of my classes at school there was a discussion about nobility and its relationship to suffering. There's an idea that to suffer is noble. I'm wondering what you have to say about this.

AH: Nobility and suffering? Well, let's see. Here we look at everything from the perspective of what is real in us, Essence. The most important thing is to see and value our essential selves. So when we look at any issue—such as nobility and suffering, pride, humility, courage—we always consider it from the perspective of Essence. If we look at it from the perspective of the superego or the personality, it will appear very complicated. We would never find an answer, because there are no answers from the perspective of personality. From the perspective of Essence, things are much simpler and clearer. Only the perspective of essential truth will give us the understanding we need for our work here.

We can look at nobility and suffering from this perspective and see where it leads. I see that nobility has to do with being and acting according to the truth of Essence. But let's look first at the common ideas about nobility. What are the connotations of this word? What is nobility usually associated with?

S: Kings.

AH: Kings. What else?

S: Graciousness.

AH: Graciousness. What else?

S: Being born into it.

AH: Being born into it. Right.

S: Enlightened judgment. Supposedly, the nobles lead the country and make the laws.

S: Courage.

S: They're supposed to have better breeding.

AH: Better breeding? So it seems that nobility is associated in our minds with royalty and with the behavior we think should come with this. It is associated with kings and queens, princes and princesses, nobles. I think that's a good way to look at it. The king or the queen. A story that looks at this from the perspective of Essence is "The King's Son," in Idries Shah's book *Tales of the Dervishes*. It says that we're royal born.

From the perspective of Essence, nobility is to be and act from the truth of Essence, to be a person living in accord with the truth. It is understood that a person of noble character doesn't let social or political pressures sway him. In that respect, to be noble is to not let your superego (the part of you that's always judging you critically) or other people's superegos sway you, but to act according to the real truth.

There can be a kind of suffering involved in this way of living. We will discuss that shortly. For now, we see that if suffering is in the service of Essence, if it is part of seeing the truth and acting according to the truth, then the suffering is noble. If the suffering is because of your superego's demands and expectations or because of any rejection of reality, it is not noble. It is ignoble.

Let us look at the nature of ignoble suffering from the perspective of Essence. Suffering always arises when you are out of contact with Essence or seeking something other than Essence. If you value anything—husbands, wives, children, girlfriends, parents, jobs, money, sports, cars, anything at all—over what is true in you, there is suffering. Automatically, that movement outwards (seeking satisfaction from external reality) wounds you. It is a wound to your heart. It is not that the factors of our external lives or our human desires are antithetical to our Work. Like everything else, they can be respected and understood for what they are. But if they come *before* Essence, there will be suffering, pain, frustration, and anger.

It is important to understand this; it is not easy to see things this way. When we begin to work on ourselves and to know our essence, we are usually not doing it for the sake of Essence itself, but with hopes for getting this or that—to become more beautiful, more loving, more "spiritual," to get people to like us. You might believe that if you develop your essence, you'll get a better mate or have more money. If you're working from that perspective, who's doing it? Who's acting? It's not Essence. It's your unconscious, so it will automatically bring suffering. The posture itself is a posture of deficiency, which is always a posture of pain. The body will automatically contract, be wounded. It will lose its joy and happiness.

I don't mean that we shouldn't want anything besides Essence. Not at all. If that's what I meant, then we would be somewhere in the desert, being monks and nuns, wearing white robes and long strings of beads. That is not what I mean. What is meant is that Essence should be the primary concern in our lives. Everything else should come second and should function in the service of Essence. You need to do whatever in your life will enhance and support your essence. Whatever it is, absolutely. That is the true source of rules, the source of morality and right conduct. It is the rule for nobility in living. Sometimes it looks like the person living this way is suffering, not going after the satisfactions that most people associate with happiness. The reality is that when life is lived in this way, there is a satisfaction and joy beyond anything the personality can experience.

Most people say they want to feel good; they want to feel happy and have a good time. They go after illusory satisfactions that only increase their suffering. If a person really wants to be happy, then she should go about it in the right way—which is to value Essence over everything else. If you do that, you are happy. If you don't, you are not. It's that simple. If you continually say, "My boyfriend is the most important thing in my life; I'll do anything not to lose him," then you prefer him to your own essence and you will suffer. This is true even if you stay in bed with him twenty-four hours a day, even if he adores you. If that is your highest preference, you will suffer. You won't even be able to properly enjoy him because your heart will be closed since you are turned away from yourself. You will, of course, be afraid of losing him. It is very simple: If you go that way, you will be in hell; if you go the way of Essence, you will be in heaven. Most people who want heaven choose the way to hell. They wonder, when they get there, why this 'heaven' doesn't feel so good.

Many of us prefer not to believe the principle that preferring anything over Essence leads to suffering. We can try to change this fact, to get around it, but it won't change.

It's a law of nature, as basic as the law that rain falls downward. We may try to cheat this law, convincing ourselves that we are living for Essence when our real motivations are different. But you cannot cheat Essence; it will not work.

One reason we don't want to see this truth is that we often believe that if we choose to live in accordance with the truth of Essence, we will lose all the goodies of life that we're attached to. We are so accustomed to looking at our lives from the perspective of getting things from the outside, we believe that if we cease to count on this pattern, we will lose them all. This is not so. In fact, if all your actions and desires, all the aspects of your life are subordinated to the truth of Essence, you can have what you want in your life. You can be famous, rich, sexy, have a family, a career, all these things. And you can enjoy them in the fullness of Essence, rather than always trying to get more and fearing the loss of what you have. There is no conflict between living the essential life and getting what you want in the world. In fact, when we are living according to our essence, it is possible finally to love our lives and the things in our lives. But if we value external things over our essence, then we shut off the part that can enjoy these things. The heart of joy, what we call *the yellow heart* or *the bright sun*, becomes sunny when it is turned toward Essence. When it is turned somewhere else, it is dark. It's that simple.

This doesn't mean that we should feel bad because we don't always turn our hearts toward Essence. That will close our hearts even more. What we can do is to see the truth of how we turn away from ourselves. We can see what makes us turn away from the truth. We can see that unconsciously we believe something else will work. We can then understand that belief and see why we believe it. When we see that completely, we don't need to do it any more. It's not a matter of whipping ourselves into line. It's a matter of seeing and understanding how we are not in line, how

we are not in harmony with the truth. The more we understand, the more we are aligned with the truth. The more
we are aligned with the truth, the more joy we will find,
the more happiness, love, fulfillment, and satisfaction. We
can become deeply content simply by being in harmony with
the truth.

Most people don't understand this. They think they can
achieve contentment, love, and happiness by getting this
or that. They want the right kind of body, the right kind
of lover, the right house. When you see what you can experience in the realm of Essence, you see that these things are
peanuts. Absolutely nothing. It's a degradation of human
life to prefer these things over what is possible for Essence.
When you align yourself with the truth, then beauty,
majesty, nobility, fullness, pleasure, joy, and love are all
available to you. The more you see your essence, the more
you see that what you wanted before was nothing. When
you get deeper and deeper into your essence, you enter into
the universal levels of essential reality where the beauty,
fulfillment, and possibility are beyond human imagination. There is no way for the mind to grasp it.

As you actualize your Personal Essence, you can bring
that fullness into your life. Then everything in your life—
your work, your job, your relationship with your lover, children, friends—can become filled with Essence rather than
substituting for Essence. The point is to realize Essence in
your life; that's why we're here. We're not here to suffer.
We're not here just to work or raise children. We're here
to completely fulfill our potential. We are here to learn what
it's like to be really human. It is very rare to know what
it's like to be a complete, mature human being.

Fulfilling desires that arise from the unconscious is not the
same fulfillment as we experience in essential life. The unconscious believes that fulfillment has to do with what others
give us, think of us, or feel toward us. The unconscious is

rarely focused on *being* itself. It is focused on the mind's desires, expectations, projections, and memories.

When we look at the deepest level, what is actually there? Existence, presence. Existence and presence are not the focus of the unconscious or the ego. But Essence knows what is there; Essence knows what is real. When you feel happy, it has nothing to do with what others think of you or what you think of yourself, whether you're good or bad, big or small, sexy, ugly, smart, stupid. If you're happy, you're happy—that's it. If you're valuable, you're valuable. Your being is unconditional.

The unconscious, on the other hand, works on the basis that in order to feel certain ways, certain things have to happen. "If you love me, then I'll be happy. If you don't love me, then I'll be miserable." Everything is conditional. When happiness is essential, it's not like that. If you love me, I'll feel one kind of happiness; if you don't, I'll feel a different kind. It's just a variation. If I am by myself in my room reading my book, that's a certain kind of happiness. If I am in bed with a woman, it's another kind of happiness. If I am sleeping and not aware of any book or any woman, it's yet another kind of happiness. If I'm working, it's another kind of happiness still. They're all wonderful, all good.

Being noble, living according to the truth, will get you to this place. You need to be willing to let go of everything— everything you have, everything you believe, every idea you have about yourself and everyone else, every feeling. Without this, you are filled with ideas, desires, and attachments instead of yourself. You must be willing to let go of them in order to see the truth. At the deeper stages, you have to let go of even your body, even pleasure and happiness, for the sake of truth. You need to let them go so that Essence can fill you.

From this discussion, we can see that there is a kind of sacrifice to be made for the essential life, and this sacrifice, this putting the truth before everything else, can involve a certain suffering. This is another connection between nobility and suffering. Yet what is really going on is that suffering is being exposed. Nobility involves forbearance for the truth. In the Work, people sometimes go through intense pain and suffering, exposing the lies of the personality and seeing the truth of the suffering that is already there. It is not that suffering is noble in itself or valuable to the Work as such. We suffer because we are not in touch with ourselves; often we are not even in touch with our suffering. We can see our suffering as noble if it is part of our movement toward our essential selves, toward the truth. Nobility is valuing the truth even if it includes suffering, valuing the truth over the distractions and external values we try to substitute for Essence. Thus nobility might involve a kind of suffering, but when you move toward the truth, the fulfillment and joy of Essence make you see that what you valued before was nothing.

We're deeply conditioned to expect fulfillment, nourishment, and pleasure from the outside. It is one of our deepest conditionings. Does anyone know what the first conditioning was? What first predisposed you toward believing that you can get what you want from the outside?

S: Nourishment?

AH: What do you mean by "nourishment?"

S: Even as an embryo, the food that sustains us comes from outside.

AH: Exactly. As an embryo, we were completely dependent on the outside. We actually had an umbilical cord feeding us. That total dependence continued for the first few years of our lives. It is deeply ingrained in the body and mind, and we continue to act according to that conditioning. We still behave like embryos. That conditioning is so deep because it happened at a time when you didn't even know you existed. It is in your cells and your bones. But it can be exposed and understood.

So the choice is between two things: to be an embryo or an adult of the species. On the whole earth, there are very few representatives of the adult of the species. The adult is awesome. We all have a chance to be that. An embryo doesn't have to stay in the embryonic state; it can develop. Most of the time we don't actually live as embryos, but we think as embryos. We believe we are embryos, and we behave as if we get all our love and nourishment from outside. Our embryonic minds need to grow up, and it is useful to notice when we act like embryos and when we act like adults.

Of course there is nothing wrong with getting things from outside, but you can also be complete in your own being. We are not making a moral judgment or rejecting being embryonic; it's just a limitation we need to go through. If we remain stuck in this state, a great deal of suffering will result.

Noble suffering, ultimately, is really nothing but the sacrifice of the unconscious, so that the Personal Essence can sit on the throne of truth, wearing the robe of peace.

SIX

Value

A H Almaas: What is the value of the Work for you?
S: I think the real value is in things I don't really
know about yet, but I do feel value when I recognize states like being joyful. Recently a friend said to me,
"You have everything," but that is a sort of incidental
value. As I clear up my personality issues, I can get the things
I really value. The real value is a state of being.

S: I've been thinking about the question of value in connection with courses I'm taking in philosophy. I feel that
I've been thrown a lifeline from non-being to existence. It's
about knowing that *I am*, that there is a purpose to my life
other than just floating around on earth for a while and
being uptight. There is a reality now. I still resist, but I feel
that I have a focus, a reason to live.

AH: You're finding that there is a reason to live.

S: There is a reason for *me* to live. Now I have an opportunity to learn how to live life fully.

S: I see people around me who are lost, suppressing themselves. The Work has taught me what I'm suppressing. There is a path to myself. A lot of things that could be important aren't that important. When I get something now, it means less, yet I enjoy it more. That's a real freedom.

S: My thoughts about the value of the Work involve a theme about freedom. I have a conscious choice now whether or not to have fun. I can go about my daily life with joy, a sense of freedom, or I can worry or hassle. Part of me knows that hassles are unnecessary; they're tied up with wanting. If I allow it, there is a very joyful way to live. I have the freedom to get what I want.

S: I, too, feel that life has a different meaning than before. I thought I would have a relationship, a job, a house, children, and that would be my life. Now there's so much more. I feel that there are no limits to my life; I can have anything I want. Just learning to understand what's going on is rewarding.

S: There are many valuable things I've received from the Work. What stands out is a sense of strength. I can also see previously hidden parts of myself; there's something there besides what I thought was there. I have many pleasures I never thought were possible.

S: I've gained a sense of glory.

AH: Yes, glorious presence. So there are lots of truths here. I will add some things now to bring it all together. There are three components to the question, "What is the value of the Work for you?" They are *value*, the *Work*, and *you*. What is value? What is the Work? And what are you? I can say it in one simple sentence: Value, the Work, and you are one thing. It's all value. The Work is value, and you are value.

Let's talk about what we usually take the word "value" to mean. For most people, value is the value of the superego. What the superego approves of, you take to be of value. What the superego disapproves of, you take to be not valuable. So value generally depends a lot on our unconscious, our conditioning, and our beliefs. What we give value to at the beginning of the Work depends on our unconscious motivations. One of you said the things that were important to you before don't seem that important now, so the things that you value have changed.

Earlier, you might have valued something because of a certain unconscious deficiency you feel. If you didn't feel beautiful, for example, you might have placed a lot of value on having more beauty. I'm not saying that beauty is not valuable, but in this case, valuing it comes from a sense of deficiency. That's how we usually approach value. Or perhaps we value the things that gave us pleasure in childhood.

From this perspective, what governs most valuing is seeking pleasure and avoiding pain. Anything that helps you avoid pain is valued. That means that all your defense mechanisms and resistances are valued highly. At the beginning of the Work, you put up a big fight to keep them. You've spent years building up all your ideas of how you are, how you should be, and how the world should be. These long-cherished dreams are based mostly on experiences of deficiency in childhood. As you understand yourself more through the Work and as you see what is really of value to you, these desires and expectations will change.

So far, we are not addressing the question "What is value?" but examining what is seen as valuable to us in ordinary life. One thing we can observe about our values is that they change over time. You might fall in love, feel that you value someone, and two years later you don't like him any more. You don't value him the way you used to;

maybe you value someone else more. Did the person change? Not necessarily; maybe not at all. So what changed his value for you?

Or maybe you liked Mexican food for a long time, and now you like French food. What changed the value of these things for you? Clearly, a shift in value doesn't depend on the object itself. The food didn't change. Although we usually think that the object itself has value, we can easily see that it's not so. Value is something we attach to an object. We determine what we value, and our values change as we change, not as the objects change. Since value is something we attribute to objects, people, or activities, it must be something arising in us.

What is this something in you that when you attach it to objects, people, or activities, it makes them valuable? Suppose you value football, and during football season, you're glued to the TV watching all the games. What is the value you give football? Is it an idea, concept, belief, a feeling you have about it, or is it something else? According to what we've said, value will arise in most people according to a certain belief or a certain feeling. Maybe you like football because your father liked football. Maybe you want to be part of a special group of people who like football. If you played football as a child with your father or with a friend, you might like football. These clearly are motivations from the past that cause you to value something, but these causes are not the value itself. They are simply what make you put value in a particular place. So what is this value you give to things?

S: I would say that I put value on something that matches a feeling I have inside, like pleasure.

AH: Yes, we generally value things that give us pleasure, but sometimes we value things that don't give us pleasure. How many people value their little games, even though they know that they always bring pain and suffering?

We're trying to disentangle value from the objects of value and the motivations for value. We want to go to the source of value. If we see this, maybe we'll have more freedom about what we value. We want to understand what it is in us that values.

S: When I value something and am very interested in it, it brings out a certain energy in me.

AH: What is this energy? It's true that an object you value will bring out a certain energy that you like. But we see that the object is chosen by you, not the other way around. That's a measure of freedom that we have and don't usually see. We think, "If I get this, I will be happy." We don't see that we've made a choice to value that thing. What we want to do here is learn to free ourselves from the objects of value, to find out what value is so we can put value on things according to what is best for us, not according to our unconscious conditioning.

Let's go back to what some of you said. Jeff said that he used to value cars, motorcycles, his job; then he discovered that what he valued was a state of being. This is something we rarely realize: What we value is the state of being itself. It is *being,* not some idea about who we are. Usually we value ourselves only when we approve of ourselves. "If I am beautiful, I am valuable." "If somebody loves me, I'm valuable." "If I'm smart, I'm valuable." I've seen that for many of you, value is in inverse proportion to weight! These are some of the criteria we have for valuing ourselves. Yet as Jeff said, there is something else— which is not to value yourself for a particular reason, but to value yourself for just being. To value that you exist, that you are. To value the fact of you. It is possible to value just being who you are, at any moment, and not to value yourself because you exist, but to know that existence itself is value.

S: For me, value is still attached to certain feelings.

AH: Yes, many of you have moved from valuing external things to valuing internal things. We can come to value certain emotions—feeling kind, feeling good, or even feeling angry. It is true that valuing these internal states might be deeper or more durable than valuing a car that makes you feel a certain way. You're valuing the feeling itself. But you don't need to make valuing yourself dependent on certain feelings. That would be relating to feelings the same way that you relate to external values. For example, you might say, "I like the feeling of love and merging. I don't like the feeling of independence." But that is just like any other conditional valuing. It is possible to go beyond this, to get to a place where the value is just there, not a consequence of something. Real value depends on nothing. Now we're getting close to what value is. What is it in you that exists as value? What is it in you that you put on other things that gives them value?

S: Sometimes it feels like a substance. When I value myself, I feel I *am* value.

AH: Right. That's what we're talking about—existence itself. It is not valuable; it *is* value. It is the source of value. It is what makes anything else have value.

Value is an aspect of Essence. It can be experienced as absolute value. Some of you have experienced this. Your value is independent of what your mind says. It is independent of what your superego or anybody else's superego says. It is independent of what happens. Your value is independent of whether you are married or single, whether you have one car or ten cars or a bicycle, whether someone loves you or not, whether you're happy or unhappy, dead or alive, sick or healthy. Value, existing as value, is separate from these things.

So this is one of the ways we can experience Essence— as value itself. Value can exist without any object. *I am* Value. That is how Essence manifests. All the qualities of

Essence are fundamental on this level, just as Truth, for Essence, is not truth *about* something; it exists *as* Truth.

Value. You can feel it, be it, see it, smell it, taste it. Value is quite palpable. It is you. It is your essence.

So, the value of the Work for you is to realize this Value, to see your own value, to see yourself as Value. The Work itself, beyond and behind its methods and structures, *is* that Value, is Essence itself, because Essence is the source of the Work. The Work is not valuable; the Work is Value. In time you will see that you are not valuable; you are Value itself.

S: Is Value the same as Love?

AH: They're all Essence, each with a different flavor. Each is like a whole universe, reflected in a different facet of a diamond. So just as Love and Truth are both Essence, each with different flavors, Love and Value reflect the same essential reality in different flavors.

S: All this exists whether we're experiencing it or not?

AH: Of course. It's your nature. The Work is to be aware of that nature, to do whatever is necessary to be aware of that part of you. It is said that Essence exists whether you are aware of it or not. This is true, but not completely true. When you are aware of Essence, it is more present. If you are not aware of it, it is hidden inside you, just a little flame keeping you alive. For some people, it is in their minds; for some, in their hearts; for some, in their bellies or in their spines. When you become aware of Essence, it comes out. It fills you. You can *be* it then.

S: Does everybody have Essence?

AH: The way I see it, it's not possible to be alive without Essence. Essence is the source of life.

Let's go back to the question of value. Now that we see a glimpse of what value is, we can reconsider the question, "What is the value of the Work for you?" I think we can get a better idea now of the purpose or the value of the Work. It's much more fundamental than how we usually think of it, more basic. The Work is to realize who you are. And who you are, from one perspective, is value.

So looking for value is looking for oneself. People ask, "What is the meaning of life? What is the value of life?" The answer is not in words. When you see yourself as Value, it becomes much easier to let Essence really unfold in its beauty, its majesty, its grandeur, with its pleasures and joys. When you experience Value in yourself, you will see that Value is the ground, the basis, of what we call the Personal Essence, what is in you that *is* you. You are based in Value.

Value is so definite, so palpable, that it has a color, a taste, and a texture. As you have seen, Essence has these qualities of color, taste, and texture. Value is a beautiful amber color; its taste is delicious. When you experience yourself as Value, you'll see that you are delicious. Value is like an exotic, precious dessert.

Just as when we look for truth, we look first at the lies, in exploring Value, we look at our lack of self esteem, our feelings of inferiority or deficiency. By understanding these we can finally get to value-as-such. I think many people here know what Value is at this moment; it is in the air.

SEVEN

Truth and Compassion

A H Almaas: Today I want to discuss the relationship between truth and compassion. It should be useful to everyone. We'll elucidate the meaning and significance of each of these concepts. Before we go on, does anyone here know the color associated with compassion?

S: Green.

AH: It's important to know that, so that we can understand this story. In Sufi lore *Khidr* means "the green one." You have heard the story before, but today we'll look at it from a different perspective. It's called, "The Land of Truth."

The Land of Truth

A certain man believed that the ordinary waking life, as people know it, could not possibly be complete.

81

He sought the real Teacher of the Age. He read many books and joined many circles, and he heard the words and witnessed the deeds of one master after another. He carried out the commands and spiritual exercises which seemed to him to be most attractive.

He became elated with some of his experiences. At other times he was confused; and he had no idea at all of what his stage was, or where and when his search might end.

This man was reviewing his behaviour one day when he suddenly found himself near the house of a certain sage of high repute. In the garden of that house he encountered Khidr, the secret guide who shows the way to Truth.

Khidr took him to a place where he saw people in great distress and woe, and he asked who they were. "We are those who did not follow real teachings, who were not true to our undertakings, who revered self-appointed teachers," they said.

Then the man was taken by Khidr to a place where everyone was attractive and full of joy. He asked who they were. "We are those who did not follow the real Signs of the Way," they said.

"But if you have ignored the Signs, how can you be happy?" asked the traveler.

"Because we chose happiness instead of Truth," said the people, "just as those who chose the self-appointed chose also misery."

"But is happiness not the ideal of man?" asked the man.

"The goal of man is Truth. Truth is more than happiness. The man who has Truth can have whatever mood he wishes, or none," they told him. "We have pretended that Truth is happiness, and happiness Truth, and people have believed us, therefore you, too, have until now imagined that happiness must be the same as Truth. But happiness makes you its prisoner, as does woe."

Then the man found himself back in the garden, with Khidr beside him.

"I will grant you one desire," said Khidr.

"I wish to know why I have failed in my search and how I can succeed in it," said the man.

"You have all but wasted your life," said Khidr, "because you have been a liar. Your lie has been in seeking personal gratification when you could have been seeking Truth."

"And yet I came to the point where I found you," said the man, "and that is something which happens to hardly anyone at all."

"And you met me," said Khidr, "because you had sufficient sincerity to desire Truth for its own sake, just for an instant. It was that sincerity, in that single instant, which made me answer your call."

Now the man felt an overwhelming desire to find Truth, even if he lost himself.

Khidr, however, was starting to walk away, and the man began to run after him.

"You may not follow me," said Khidr, "because I am returning to the ordinary world, the world of lies, for that is where I have to be, if I am to do my work."

And when the man looked around him again, he realized that he was no longer in the garden of the sage, but standing in the Land of Truth. (Idries Shah, *Thinkers of the East*, pp. 66–67)

I keep rereading this story—just as I've read it to you many times—because it is the single most important truth we have to work with and because it is a truth that people keep forgetting. Not only is it the single most important truth, it is also the most practical truth, the most helpful truth, and the best advice I could ever give you for absolutely all situations.

As Khidr said, he lives in the ordinary world, what he calls "the world of lies" where everybody embraces their lies and turns away from the truth about themselves and others. We have a tendency to regard truth as our enemy, and we usually think that lies are our friends. We try to avoid truth at all costs because we think truth will hurt. We think that truth will take things away from us, that truth will deprive us of things, that truth will put us in unpleasant situations, so we try to protect ourselves by using lies. When we do that, we live the life of lies; we live in the world of lies.

So let's see more about truth, lies, compassion, and the relationships between them. I think we know more about lies than anything else. Everyone's an expert at lying to himself and others. We've been doing it for years and years. It's important to see the attitude we usually hold, which is that truth is our enemy. That's why there are such things as avoidance, repression, and resistance. If we didn't think truth was our enemy, we wouldn't resist and repress our emotions; we wouldn't try to avoid seeing the truth. But usually we aren't aware of the fact that we reject the truth and fight it. If you can see that you resist truth, already one layer of the lie is removed.

If you look at the work you've done in this group so far, it's essentially uncovering the lies and seeing the truth. We understand that the lies of the personality provide valuable clues to the hidden truths of Essence. I don't need to say much to you about the importance of the truth for understanding oneself, one's realization, or one's freedom. We all know that, even though our unconscious may still resist.

I think you also know the importance of compassion. Let's talk a little more about what compassion means. Usually compassion is seen as a desire to alleviate someone else's pain; compassion is experienced as the desire to help. We feel compassionate when we see someone hurt. Rarely do we feel compassionate when someone isn't hurting. So we connect compassion with pain and hurt. However, this is only the elementary level of compassion—emotional compassion.

Remember the story. Khidr, the green one, is the symbol of compassion. Was it his role to alleviate pain? What did he do?

S: He told the truth.

AH: Yes, he told the truth. And that's the real function of compassion. The point of compassion is not to eliminate suffering, but to lead a person to the truth so that she will be able to live the life of truth. This is an important fact that we tend to not see because our ideas about compassion are not accurate. Look for yourself. What kind of compassion have you believed in and acted from? For most of us, it's obvious where our prejudice lies. Our compassion has not been on the side of truth; it has been on the side of feeling good. This is not the compassion of Essence; it is the compassion of emotions. It is understandable that it hurts to see someone hurting. You may also feel compassionate towards yourself when you are hurting; this compassion helps. So what is the relationship between hurt, truth and compassion?

Compassion is a kind of healing agent that helps us tolerate the hurt of seeing the truth. The function of compassion in the Work is not to reduce hurt; its function is to lead to the truth. Much of the time, the truth is painful or scary. Compassion makes it possible to tolerate that hurt and fear. It helps us persist in our search for truth. Truth will ultimately dissolve the hurt, but this is a by-product and not the major purpose of compassion.

In fact, it is only when compassion is present that people allow themselves to see the truth. Where there is no compassion, there is no trust. If someone is compassionate toward you, you trust him enough to allow yourself to be vulnerable, to see the truth rather than reject it. The compassion doesn't alleviate the pain; it makes the pain meaningful, makes it part of the truth, makes it tolerable.

This way of viewing compassion makes a tremendous difference in our lives. Seeing compassion as a guide to the truth rather than something to alleviate hurt can change the way we behave toward ourselves, our friends, everyone.

It may seem like a subtle difference, but one perspective will take you away from truth and the other will take you towards it. One will keep you unconscious, and the other will help you learn the truth.

Generally, we protect ourselves from pain and fear and from our unconscious to protect ourselves from the truths in our unconscious. This also "protects" us from the truth of who we are, from our Essence. Believing we are acting compassionately, we try to protect others from the same. But is that compassionate? We spend our lives trying to protect the people closest to us from the truth because we think they will be hurt. We also protect ourselves from the truth because we think we will hurt. We think it will be too much for us.

We're not saying that the emotional kind of compassion—wanting to alleviate your own or someone else's suffering—is bad. Especially when you begin to work on understanding yourself, this kind of compassion can be beneficial and useful. But if what you are interested in is your essence, emotional compassion can be a barrier.

To get to Essence, you must work with true compassion, the door to the truth. It is not a matter of seeking misery or seeking happiness. As the story said, the point is the truth. It is amazing to look at our lives and see how much we act from the perspective of seeking happiness rather than truth, which is the perspective of emotional compassion. We can see, for instance, how we try to protect our parents from the truth of who we are. We may ask, "How can I be happy? My mother isn't, so how can I be without making her feel more miserable?" or "How can I be strong if my father is sitting there being weak—won't he feel humiliated?" So we push the truth of our own experience of happiness or strength away from us in order to not cause pain to our parents. So in a sense, we do it out of compassion, the compassion of a child who sees hurt and can't tolerate causing it or adding to it. From that time on, we believe that compassion is a kind of protection, protection of the ones we love. That's how it starts—the burying of the truth and of our essence.

There's another interesting relationship between truth, pain, and compassion. Most of you who have learned to experience compassion have seen that it usually opens when you allow yourself to experience pain, and that pain usually comes by seeing the truth about yourself or your situation. When you see the truth, you feel hurt, and when you allow yourself to feel the hurt, compassion comes. If you don't allow yourself to feel hurt, you can't feel compassion. That's how our organism functions.

So there is a reciprocal relationship between truth and compassion, and there is a connection between these things and suffering. The suffering is not the point; suffering is something in between that we go through. From the perspective of Essence, it is irrelevant. The important part is truth—the truth about who we are—no matter how much hurt, suffering, and fear it takes to get there. Sometimes the pain is there so that the person will learn the truth.

Did I tell you the story about the student who was taking care of an older woman who was dying? She is a student I see weekly. Week after week, she came to me crying, suffering, talking about the old woman in the hospital who had suffered so much in her life and how she was always in pain now. Every week the student would come and cry about this woman. When the old woman finally died, the student cried even more and was angry at God. Suffering with pain, she asked, "What's it for?" Good question. There is an interesting answer: The old woman taught the student compassion. Through knowing the old woman, the student's heart opened, and she experienced as she never had before the green subtlety the Sufis recognize as compassion. The suffering led to the opening of her heart, which is necessary to allow Essence. The old woman also learned what compassion was through the student.

From the perspective of the universal level of Essence, what happens in terms of the difficulties of our lives—or the happiness and joy—are not as important as the development of Essence. Our whole lives are for that. From this perspective we see that it is not the truth which actually brings suffering, but the lies. The suffering is already there as a result of the lies. The truth simply exposes it. When the suffering is exposed, the person can let go of it. So the truth is compassionate in that way. It can eliminate suffering by exposing the lies that actually cause it.

As you know more completely what compassion is and what truth is, you will see that compassion is the door to the truth. You will go through all kinds of suffering, and compassion will keep the door open for you. You will see that on the other side of the door is a state of Essence that is truth. It is Essence as truth.

This brings us to the question "What is truth?" Let's begin, again, with the ordinary sense of truth, the one we understand at the beginning of our Work. Usually we see truth as a characteristic of a statement or a perception. We say, "This statement is true," or "This statement is not true," or "This perception is true," or "This perception is not true." This is the ordinary understanding of truth. When we work on our unconscious, finding the truth means finding out what is actually there, discovering our actual beliefs, our unconscious motivations and conflicts.

First we see the truth of our defenses, the lies we believe in. We see that they exist, and we begin to identify them. Through observing our lies, we can see the deficiencies we feel underneath the lies. We discover how often we consciously believe the opposite of our unconscious beliefs and feelings. We unconsciously feel we are weak, and so we create a lie in the form of a belief that we are strong. Because we may even believe that we feel strong, it will be difficult to uncover the feeling of weakness. It is important that compassion be present for that to happen.

Let's look for a moment at your actual experience when you're going through a lot of pain in the process of seeing the truth about yourself. Why do you go through all this pain? When people come here to do the Work, they tell me, "What I want is to get rid of this difficulty. I want a boyfriend. I want a new job. I want a new car. I want to stop being afraid all the time." But when you are actually going through the Work, when you are suffering, are you thinking, "I am doing this because I want to get rid of my fear"? Are you thinking, "I am going through this because I want to get a girlfriend or a boyfriend"? Is that what happens? A lot of the time, when you really get into it, that is not what happens. You forget about all these things. There is a very strong motivation that says, "I want to experience this." What is that desire? Where does it come from?

When you really get into seeing things about yourself, it's very painful. You say, "Oh, am I really that jealous?" or "Am I really that dependent, or that angry?" You don't like it, but something in you says, "I want to feel this and get to the bottom of it." Nobody's making you do it. In that moment, what is compelling you? In the middle of the experience, it's no longer the motivation you thought you had; that motivation is not in your mind any more. What is motivating you is your desire to see the truth. Seeing the truth becomes fulfilling in itself; it seems to bring some subtle pleasure and joy. So you want to see the truth regardless of how difficult it is.

So looking at this experience can take us closer to what truth is. It is no longer a question of what is a true statement or perception. There is something more. It is, in a sense, that the truth wants itself. When the truth is manifesting, you want it. Essence wants to realize itself, and the more truth there is, the more it is realized. When you're working in this way, the impulse comes from such a deep place that you don't even think about it. You are just attracted. That's what is called "the love of truth for its own sake." You want it not because you want to get rid of your fear, or to achieve this or that, but simply because you want to possess the truth. The truth itself is what you want. It is such a deep, compelling desire that when it is there, nothing can stand in its way. You might be in the middle of tremendous pain, but somehow the truth makes you go through it, and it's fine.

We all have that impulse, but usually we cover it up. Only at those times when we really get into the reality of what's happening do we have that sense of truth. With the truth, we have a sense that we're more real, more here, that reality is more here, that there is something here that is significant, meaningful, life-fulfilling, regardless of whether it's joyful or painful. Because it is the truth. Our experience becomes pregnant with something. There is a fullness, a satisfaction, that doesn't come any other way. There's a part of us that is more here. Everything around us seems more real, more concrete, more embodied.

These moments cannot be logically explained; you know them only by tasting them. They are clues to something about truth. The more truth we are experiencing, the more the sense exists that "Yes, there is something here that I want." Now, what is it about the truth that we want?

As we get more present in our bodies, in our bellies, we get closer to our essence which is truth. This is what allows us to know what is true and what is false, not from logical deduction or from the unconscious. You just know. You are close to that subtle sense that is truth. After a while you see that, for you, truth is no longer a judgment of certain situations or statements; it has an existence of its own. Essence is truth then, and you will know where the satisfaction and joy have been coming from every time you feel the truth in you. All this work we do on seeing the truth has been to lead to that truth, the truth of Essence.

As we have said, the process of learning to see the truth will bring up a lot of pain, fear, and humiliation. When you are faced with the choice of seeing the truth about yourself or someone else, or avoiding the pain, which is the compassionate action? If you choose to hide the truth in any situation, no matter how devastatingly painful it might be to face, you are sentencing yourself to living in the world of lies.

So you see, there is a beautiful cause-and-effect relationship between truth and compassion. They go together. Compassion leads to truth, truth to compassion. What makes us avoid either or both of them is usually pain. We want to feel good. We want to protect our beliefs, our ideas about who we are. We want to protect ourselves from seeing the truth about others. We all have these cherished beliefs about who we are, who others are, how things are, how things are supposed to be. Seeing through these can bring fear and pain. But that is because we believe the lies. We think the lies are the truth because we don't trust the truth. But the truth itself is the point, regardless of whether or not it accords with our beliefs.

You see in your work on yourself that the truth is often not in accord with what you believe about yourself. A lot of you have discovered, for instance, what love is. It's not what you thought. When you discovered value, it wasn't what you thought. When you felt fulfillment, it wasn't what you thought. This letting go of what you thought— it was painful, wasn't it? It was scary. You fought tooth and nail. "No! I won't let go of that one!" But the more you let go, the more you experienced the real thing.

It's interesting too that compassion goes along with trust. Trust and compassion are almost the same. A lot of the time we don't trust the truth, but the truth is the best thing for us. When we don't trust the truth, we don't have compassion for ourselves.

Dedicating ourselves to seeing this truth and living according to it means going all the way. All the way to the knowledge that truth is truth, regardless of your situation, regardless of whether you like it or not. The fact that it scares you won't make it false. What is, *is*. Who we are, the way reality is, that's just the way it is. If you are compassionate toward yourself, you will let yourself see that truth. The Work and life itself are a matter of seeing the truth, knowing the truth, and being the truth. There is something about the life of truth, the life of Essence, the meaningfulness of it, the significance of it, the depth of it, the subtle, intrinsic joy and satisfaction of it that when you experience it, you don't want anything else. You are willing to see through anything to have the truth. It is closer to who you are than anything else.

We usually want to hold on to our beliefs and conceptions of ourselves, thinking that if we let them go, we will lose something we cannot live without. But when you have compassion for yourself, you begin to trust yourself. And you begin to see that it is the truth that saves you, finally.

EIGHT

Trust

AH Almaas: Today I'll ask everybody a question. The question is "What is trust?"

S: When I say to someone, "I trust you," I think what I really mean is "I trust you not to hurt me."

AH: So, for you, trust has to do with hurt, the question of getting hurt or not getting hurt.

S: For me, the word trust means feeling a sense of ground, feeling a place beneath which one cannot fall. And so if I trust somebody, it's like having somewhere to stand. In myself or somewhere.

AH: A sense of support? You equate trust with support?

S: I mean that I trust people only if I feel secure in myself. If I don't, then I don't trust them. I don't trust people if I think I can be pushed by them into a place where I could get lost and be hurt by them, in a way I can't handle.

AH: So you're saying trust depends on your state. If you feel secure in yourself, it's easy for you to trust.

S: I think of trust as being earned. If somebody has my trust, they earn it. The way it comes to mind is that for somebody to earn my trust they have to make themselves empathic to my feelings and my framework.

AH: So if they are empathic with where you are, they earn your trust. That's fine. But what is trust? We're talking about *when* we trust and *how* somebody earns it, but what is trust? When we say that someone earns your trust, what do they earn?

S: They earn a little piece of me. They earn my honesty; I'll be more real with them.

AH: They earn your honesty. So you equate trust with honesty?

S: Yes. And if you go a step beyond that, it's the opposite of being protective or being reserved.

AH: Okay. Very good. So they earn your honesty. So far, we have honesty, hurt, security—what else?

S: I think it is connected with the validity or the certainty of something. Like experiencing a certain essential quality and seeing its validity and certainty, seeing that it doesn't go away, trusting it as real.

AH: You associate trust with certainty. You're certain of something, so you trust it. Let's shed more light on this. Do you know why you didn't trust me when you began this Work?

S: Because it was an act of faith to follow what you were prescribing. I didn't have enough evidence.

AH: And now you trust me more?

S: Yes, because I'm experiencing what you were talking about and what you were asking us to accept on faith.

AH: So that gives you more trust. Now you're saying what it is that gives you trust—which is the certainty that comes from direct knowledge. What is trust itself? Everybody has talked about what supports trust so far, but we haven't really touched on what trust is. When you trust somebody, what are you doing?

S: You have faith in them.

AH: You have faith, but what does that do?

S: You open up to them in a different way than you normally do.

AH: So if you trust somebody, you open up to them.

S: If you trust, you can be real without thinking about it.

AH: So trusting, for you, means letting out what's real in you without thinking about it first, without deciding. So you just let yourself be there, without defending yourself. That's good. Does anybody have any other ideas?

S: I think of trust as being a reflection of the truth and an interaction between myself and some part of me or an interaction between myself and somebody else. It seems to involve a sense of truth in the interaction.

AH: So you're saying that trust results from a sense of truth, or is the same as a sense of truth?

S: I'm not sure that they're really distinguishable.

AH: So the sense of truth and trust are very similar.

S: Trust has to do with vulnerability, too.

AH: How so?

S: When I trust, I allow myself to be vulnerable.

AH: You allow yourself to be vulnerable. So that means you feel there's no need to defend or protect yourself. That's similar to what was said about a sense of safety.

S: Then there's the whole issue of trusting yourself.

AH: Right. There's trusting yourself, trusting somebody else, trusting an idea, trusting a circumstance. It's not always an object that we're trusting. So when you trust yourself, what does that mean?

S: It means I feel like I'm on a path to myself. I trust my life. I trust what I'm doing, when I have that sense.

S: In a sense, one learns to surrender to what's there.

AH: I see. So trusting the situation, or the person, or yourself has to do with the ability to surrender to the situation, to be open, to allow yourself to be vulnerable, to let yourself be there, to let yourself be influenced by the situation.

S: The word trust, unlike knowledge or truth, has the quality of movement in it. It's not a thing that's just there in a timeless sense. There's a sense of movement and process. It has to do with expectation. It has to do with the relationship between the eternal qualities and the temporal person, somehow. It's like the movement, the quality of the movement toward things that are timeless.

AH: So you connect it pretty much with Essence.

S: I find that the more I have my essence, the fewer people I trust.

AH: You're saying that knowing more about Essence does not necessarily lead to trusting more people. It makes your trust more discriminating.

We're getting many points of view. Let's see how we might synthesize them. It seems trust has to do with truth, certainty, surrender, with the issue of being hurt or not being hurt, and with the ability to be oneself. It is what allows us to be vulnerable. I can think of several questions from this discussion. What are the varieties or levels of trust? What is trust? What leads to trust?

First, it seems that trust has different levels and different varieties: for instance, trusting yourself, trusting somebody else, trusting a situation, trusting a certain truth, or certain knowledge, or a certain belief. The experiences of these different kinds of trust feel different. When you trust yourself, you don't feel the same as when you're trusting somebody else. When you're trusting yourself, you're more surrendered to what is happening inside you, to your own promptings, to your own truth. When you're trusting somebody else, it feels different. When you trust yourself, you don't have a feeling of surrender—you just do it. When you trust somebody else, there is more sense of surrender, allowing yourself to be vulnerable, allowing yourself to be there without needing defenses. And trusting a situation means you're feeling somewhat secure in the situation. There is a kind of security and safety that things will be okay or that what's supposed to happen is going to happen.

Maybe there is a common factor among all these kinds of trust. In trusting yourself, or somebody else, or a situation, isn't there an implied security? A sense of safety or a sense of no need to protect yourself, a sense that you are in a friendly land, not a hostile one? A sense that you can allow yourself to be whatever you are in that moment without having to be too careful, without feeling paranoid? So, trust has to do with the absence of fear and paranoia. The simplest kind of trust essentially means there's no need for fear. That wherever you are—with yourself, with somebody else—you're in good hands.

That's one way of seeing different kinds of trust. Another way is in terms of different levels. For instance, you could trust your friend not to hurt you. Right? That's the most obvious kind of trust. It would be stupid to trust somebody you know is going to hurt you. So the first level has to do with the knowledge or belief that the person is not going to hurt you; this allows you to just be there. Another level is the trust that the person wants what is best for you. That's a deeper kind of trust. It takes into consideration the fact that what is good for you may sometimes hurt. This trust comes from a perception, or a belief, or a feeling, that the person wants what is good for you. So you trust them from that level.

Then there's another level where you trust, not because you know the person isn't going to hurt you, not because you know that the person wants what's good for you, but because of what you know about the person. The person may not be concerned about hurting you or not, or about doing what's good for you. At this level, you trust because of what the person is. You have the knowledge or the feeling that the person has a kind of integrity, which has nothing to do with you, but you know it is something that is to be trusted. That's yet a deeper kind of trust. It is not a very common one, but it can exist. It can go very deep, that kind of trust. The knowledge, the integrity, the reality, the truth of a person can be so clear that you continue to trust him even if you feel hurt by him, even if you don't understand why you're being hurt. What allows this kind of trust? It involves a perception or a sense of something bigger. You might not see a specific truth about why such a person's behavior is good for you, but you might see or feel a bigger truth. Either the quality of the person or the nature of the interaction can lead to this kind of trust.

These three kinds of trust all exist in this group, at times one or the other, and sometimes all of them. Sometimes you trust me because you know I'm not going to hurt you. Sometimes you trust me because you know that even though you might feel hurt by me, you see that it's still a positive thing for you. Sometimes you might feel hurt and you don't see that it's a positive thing for you, but you continue to trust.

Let's look further into what trust is. Let's say that trust is what gives the security and the safety and the confidence to allow yourself to be open in a situation, allowing whatever is there to happen without resisting it, without having to protect or defend yourself against it. That's a good operative definition of trust for now. Within this concept of trust, there are two levels. The first level, the superficial one, is the willingness to trust. You feel no conscious resistance. You can say, "Yes, I trust. I don't want to resist you or the situation." That is one level. The deeper level is actually doing it—not resisting, even unconsciously. So the superficial level

is consciously not wanting to resist, consciously not defending, consciously feeling safe and secure enough to let yourself be open and surrender to the situation. Perhaps that's
all a person can do at a given moment, even though there
is still an unconscious distrust. On the deeper level, the person trusts all the way; even the unconscious fears are gone.
Then there's a complete openness, a complete lack of resistance, defensiveness, or protectiveness, a complete lack of
fear or paranoia, a complete surrender. Not just willingness
to surrender, but really surrendering. On the first level,
there might be a willingness to surrender, but not the capacity to surrender. On the deeper level, there is the capacity
to surrender, to be there, to yield to the situation. Does this
make sense so far?

S: I have a question. When I feel willing to trust in this
group, what seems to happen is that fear and anxiety start
to come up from my unconscious. The willingness to trust,
in itself, actually brings up the fear and anxiety.

AH: Those fears are not necessarily fear of the situation
or of me. The fear is of other feelings that may come up.
And that is the point of the trust in this situation: to be able
to allow those feelings to become conscious. When I say there
is deep trust, I don't mean that there is no fear at all. I mean
there is no fear of that person or situation. You trust it so
much that you allow other fears about other things to come
out. What happens here is that you trust me, and you allow
other fears, other feelings inside you, to come up.

S: Sometimes I feel that I have trusted, but then I pull
back to protect something in case the trust isn't going to
work out.

AH: That means you don't have trust, though you
thought you did. The third kind of trust will be like that
sometimes. As far as you know, you trust the situation. But
when you get deeply into it, you find out that because of
unconscious fears you don't really trust it.

You can begin with the superficial kind of trust and find its limit. As the Work goes on, you can learn to allow the deeper trust. The more you work on the distrust and fears and paranoia, the more you'll be able to surrender.

S: I think it's also true that you can unconsciously trust more than you consciously trust. I go around pretending to myself and others that I don't trust you, when actually my behavior indicates that I do.

AH: Yes. It can happen that you trust but don't know that you trust. You trust at the deeper level, but at the superficial level you don't trust. That might be due to a fear of trusting. It's similar to when somebody loves a person and doesn't know he does because he has a fear of loving.

Now let's say more about the nature of trust so we can connect it to what leads to or produces trust. We said trust has to do with the feeling of safety, security, and confidence in a person or a situation so that you can allow yourself to be open and without defenses, to be vulnerable, to be whoever you are. Emotionally, there is no need to fear. Mentally, there is no worry or tension or concern about the situation. There are no paranoid thoughts. The mind is at rest; the heart is at rest. You have safety in the mind, security in the heart, confidence in the kath, the belly center. There is no need for agitation or tension in any of those places. So we can see why trust is a useful and good thing. When there is no tension in the mind, heart, or solar plexus, you are in a state that is conducive to self-understanding.

When there is no trust, it is hard to be present and vulnerable. What does vulnerable mean? Vulnerable means there is a delicate kind of openness. When you trust a situation, you have no fear of the situation. As we said earlier, that allows other fears to come up from the unconscious, so in that sense, you are vulnerable. But you are also at rest on some level.

So we see that trust has to do with a kind of restfulness, a lack of tension, a lack of agitation. It has to do with relaxation, with rest in the mind, rest in the heart, rest in the solar plexus. Rest in the mind is connected with rest in the heart. Rest is the lack of a need to defend or protect. It is the ability to *be*, to have a carefree attitude about what's happening in the moment. You don't have to select or censor. The experience of the heart is of security; you can actually feel the trust. Your mind is feeling safe and restful.

This state of affairs indicates that the center we call compassion, the heart center which is experienced as green, is open in that moment. When it is open, it is very much connected to the center in the middle of the brain. The two can be considered one center. The chest is the green, and the head is the blue. The green gives the sense of security in the heart. The blue gives the sense of security in the mind. The green is security on the emotional level, and the blue is on the mental level. Trust is very much connected with the energy of kindness and compassion. When the green center is open, there is trust. When it is not open, usually there is no trust. A person might think she is trusting but wouldn't feel it. She might try to convince herself that she is trusting, but if there is no compassion present, the deep trust will not be there.

Here is the connection to safety, to the issue of hurt, and allowing ourselves to be vulnerable. When you allow yourself to be vulnerable, the compassion center is open. Don't we usually trust someone if we see that he is compassionate toward us? Love alone sometimes isn't enough to engender trust, but when a person has kindness and compassion, we respond with trust. What this means is that the green center of the other person has activated your own green center. It's the same thing, the same energy. If a person is compassionate toward you, you trust him. Trust and compassion come from the same center.

So what does it take to come from this place? Generally speaking, we trust someone when we perceive compassion and kindness in him. When you allow yourself compassion in the heart, the head center opens automatically. They become one center, and there is rest in the mind. There is no questioning or doubt. When fear is gone, the solar plexus is more open, and the will is there, giving support and confidence. So we've connected trust with compassion. That's the most obvious connection because being compassionate and being trusting are almost the same thing. They have to do with the heart center and the green energy.

Now we need to connect trust to the gold; this is the connection to truth. We can see different levels of trust as they involve or ignore the truth. For instance, a person could have the green center open all the time or most of the time. This person will tend to trust other people easily. Sometimes she will trust other people even though they are not trustworthy. You know how that is—when you trust someone and it turns out you were wrong in trusting them. That happens because the green center is open, but the head center has not opened to allow for objective trust. She has the ability to trust, but there is no wisdom, no discrimination in her trusting.

So it's possible to trust completely and be wrong. Your heart is open, but you are ignorant. If, in your childhood, you trusted people and your trust was always justified, you will tend to think you can trust everybody. So someone could come along and steal all your money because you trust unrealistically. You've learned to trust because your heart was not hurt too much. This kind of trust is a sort of blind trust. It's often based on faith. It is what helps a person be devoted to somebody or something. They have the capacity to be open in the heart and to trust, but it is based on faith. They don't actually know whether the person is to be trusted or not.

We see that in the beginning, the nature of trust has to do with the openness and kindness of the heart. When you're compassionate, it's easy to trust. And when somebody else is compassionate toward you, it's easy to trust. However, as I mentioned before, compassion is a door. It's a guide to something deeper, which is the truth. That's when trust becomes connected with truth. Then you have the capacity to trust, and this capacity is objective, based on the truth of the situation or the truth of your perception. It is based on real knowledge, direct perception, direct experience.

So, what we're saying is that the capacity to trust can be there in some people without the presence of truth. On the other hand, some people cannot trust unless there is truth. However, when there is real truth and there is also the capacity to trust, then the trust is stronger. The first person will tend to get hurt more often; the second, less often. Neither is better than the other. So ultimately trust is connected to compassion and truth—the green of compassion and the gold of truth.

There are many connections between trust and compassion and truth. Compassion can lead to truth. Truth can lead to trust. Truth can also lead to compassion towards yourself and others. Your conditioning may make it easier to experience one quality while blocking another, so that as Essence unfolds, truth may come before or after compassion and trust.

The issue of hurt enters when there is work on the truth. The compassion connected to truth is not just the compassion of wanting to help someone alleviate hurt. Compassion, in this case, means having the green center open and trusting the capacity and willingness to experience hurt in order to see the truth. The objective is the truth. Hurt is one of the things you allow yourself to experience because it is needed to be able to see the truth. So when I am compassionate toward you, it is not because I don't want you to feel hurt. The function of my compassion is to allow you to trust. The trust then allows you to experience your hurt so you can see the truth. Compassion is needed to generate the trust to allow yourself to tolerate the hurt that will help you be and see the truth. The final point is the truth. Only at the most superficial level is compassion for hurt. It is true that compassion relates to hurt, but it is in the service of truth, not in the service of eliminating hurt.

This brings us to the third level of trust that I talked about before. Remember I said there were three levels. At the first level, you trust that the person won't hurt you; at the second level, you trust the person wants your well-being; and at the third level, you have objective trust in the other person. Objective trust has to do with truth. You know that the person is objective or is dedicated to truth. When you have trust in that person, you see that the person is truthful. Because of this trust, you can let yourself feel the hurt, even though you might not see for a while that what's happening is good for you. You perceive truth. And that's the deepest kind of trust because what you sense is something about the truth that transcends hurt or no hurt, feeling good or not feeling good.

Of course, seeing the truth by itself will not necessarily bring a belief in truth. What will bring the belief is valuing truth. If you see the truth and don't value it, you will not necessarily feel a sense of openness and trust. So trust in truth comes out of valuing the truth, and this allows the green center to be open. The green center is the door to Essence which leads to deeper truth, absolute truth.

S: So trusting in truth does have a different quality. I've been thinking that at other times in my life I've felt very compassionate, through different stages of being hurt—and feeling compassionate was a very emotional thing—compassion for the world. Now, when I feel, I'm not as willing to feel compassion. I mean there's some objectivity in my compassion, and maybe that has to do with those two centers. I have some clarity that the compassion has to do with truth. And it's a different kind of thing.

AH: It is. It's more objective. In the beginning, a person could have the green center open and feel compassion toward everybody all the time. That's fine. Most of the time it's good. However, what comes at a deeper level, the more objective level, is that you recognize when you need to be emotionally compassionate toward somebody and when it's better not to be. You can become very ruthless in this objectivity and in your truth, and you might not even feel that compassionate, but it is still a deeper level of compassion. It's the compassion that transcends the feeling of compassion. It's the compassion of action then.

In the beginning, people take compassion to mean the feeling of wanting to alleviate the person's pain or take it away from them. A deeper level of compassion is taking action whether you feel inclined to or not. The third level of compassion could include hurting somebody or not taking their pain away when you see it. Sometimes they need the pain to learn something about themselves. They may need it to learn about compassion. If you take away people's hurt, they won't learn how to be compassionate. We also said the most objective compassion has to do with truth. Whether the person feels hurt or doesn't feel hurt is immaterial. The point is truth, the golden truth.

The real energy of compassion toward yourself, the real attitude of trust toward yourself transcends pain and pleasure. It's truth. What you finally trust is the truth—the truth in yourself, in somebody else, or in the situation. Truth as such. Compassion has to be according to the truth and for the truth. That's why some actions that come from the deeper level of compassion might not look compassionate to someone else or to the external world. They might even look cruel, yet they might be the most compassionate thing. Often what people want to do in such a case—to act in a way that looks compassionate—is really not compassionate.

To exercise the deeper level of compassion, you have to be in touch with the truth. When you are in touch with and embodying the truth, compassion happens automatically and naturally. It's just how you function. It doesn't matter if people are hurt or not. The point is the truth. The point is the truth and the development of Essence itself. This is the final yardstick, the most objective one. Of course, in ordinary circumstances, not hurting people is valid. Why should you do things that would hurt people? Unless they are working on themselves, pursuing the truth about themselves, they're not going to learn anything from it. You just add to their suffering.

So, as we see, trust and compassion are linked. They're almost the same thing. Compassion leads to trust, and trust leads to compassion. Both are linked to truth. Hurt and vulnerability are what happen in between. They are some of what people go through in going from trust to truth or from truth to trust.

NINE

Essence is the Life

Essence is the promise. Essence is the life. Essence is the fulfillment of all our deeper longings. Essence is the answer to all our fundamental questions, absolutely—no exceptions. This is such a fundamental point, yet at the same time, such a difficult point to understand. When you understand it, it is even more difficult to accept.

Usually, when you first come here, you are interested in getting something or in getting rid of something. That's fine. In time, by using the understanding of the Work, you will see that most of your suffering comes exactly from that attitude and it is what has to change. This Work is not for you to get this or to get rid of that. What you have to change is something more fundamental. There's another part of you that has to start functioning, not the part that wants to get or get rid of something, regardless of what it is you want to get or get rid of.

If you go deeply into yourself to understand your mind and your being and the suffering in your situation, you'll find that ultimately there is no fulfillment but to *be*, to be yourself, to be your essence. To *be* is to be free. To *be* is to be fulfilled. To *be* is to enjoy. Everything else, if it is valued more, will be a hindrance to your fulfillment and satisfaction. As I said, this is very hard to accept.

Because Essence is the fulfillment and satisfaction that everyone longs for, we call this work "Ridhwan." There is no exact translation in English for "Ridhwan," but it is close to "satisfied," "fulfilled," "contented." Ridhwan is a verbal noun in Arabic that not only means "satisfied," "fulfilled," "contented," but also means "satisfying," "fulfilling," "making content." It conveys a state and an action. Ridhwan is being that acts by its very being.

Usually we believe that if we get what we want, what the personality wants, we will be fulfilled. But fulfillment is ultimately the freedom from desires. What I am saying is that being oneself, being one's essence, free from the desires of the personality, is the fulfillment. It's not that you want your essence so you can get something else. It's not that you want your essence so that you'll get rich or fall in love and live happily ever after. It's not that your essence will enable you to have children, do special things, or be famous. If this is your attitude, the dissatisfaction and the suffering will continue because you are not seeing where fulfillment lies.

When I say this principle is absolute, I mean just that. It is absolute in the way a physical law is absolute. It has nothing to do with your opinions or your preferences. That's the way reality is; it is the truth. But we try to hedge that truth, try to change it, try to show that it's not so. What stops us from understanding and accepting this truth is lack of objectivity. We don't see things as they are. That is the main obstacle—our lack of objective perception. We see things in ways that are totally dictated by our unconscious, which means that we don't see things as they are at all, or we see them always clouded and unclear. We see things according to our fears and desires; we see what we expect to see. What we see, in fact, is only our unconscious projected onto the world. We don't see the world as it really is, we don't see others as they really are, and we don't see ourselves. Because of that, our motivation, our direction, is crooked, out of alignment. Our orientation is wrong. We try to orient ourselves according to our dreams and opinions, which are all conditioned by the unconscious.

To be objective means to see exactly what is there, exactly the way it is, regardless of how you feel about it. The difficulty is that most of the time we think we see things that way when we do not. If we did see things exactly the way they are, we would see that the only fulfillment is the life of Essence. It would be simple and obvious. How else could it be? How could I want it to be different? It is the greatest freedom.

Objectivity is an important quality of Essence itself: seeing truth as it is—not according to our desires, beliefs, or emotions. There are many reasons why we don't have objective consciousness. The existence of the personality as a whole depends upon non-objectivity. Today we will talk about one particular mechanism that sustains the illusion of personality, the mechanism of projection.

Projection is one of the main defenses we use to avoid seeing the truth inside us. Projection is usually seen in terms of negative emotions—hostility, anger, fear, jealousy, things like that. For instance, a paranoid person who appears to be scared of other people is not really scared of other people. He is angry and hostile. But instead of seeing the anger and hostility in himself, he sees it outside in other people. He thinks other people want to kill him, and so he is scared of them. The truth is that he actually has murderous feelings toward them and toward himself. That is projection, displacing what is inside you to the outside. Clearly, if you see something as outside that actually exists within you, you can't be objective. Our projections determine many of our actions, our feelings, and even our life plans. Paranoia is one of the most well-known forms of projection, but projection is prevalent in other forms. Sometimes you project your fear or jealousy so that you won't have to experience them or admit that you are feeling these things. Or you say, "Look at all these weaklings around me," when it is you who are feeling weak. Since it is hard for you to feel that, you pretend you are tough and strong. Or you can project yourself onto your child, hoping that if she fulfills your dreams, you will be fulfilled.

The roots of projection are so deep that we are usually convinced that our subjective beliefs are objective truth. "Of course people are out to get me! Can't you tell? Look at their eyes! If they're not trying to get me, how come when I was crossing a street yesterday a car almost hit me? How come the price of eggs went up just when I needed to buy two dozen?" We can always find such confirmations.

Here in the group, what we project is mostly the superego. Instead of feeling our own self-judgment and self-criticism, we believe others feel this way toward us. We think they are doing it to us; we don't see that we're the ones who are doing it.

Projection is one of the first defense mechanisms developed in infancy. Its basis is what is called the "merged state." The child is in what is called the "symbiotic stage"—between the ages of three months and nine months—when he does not experience himself as separate from his environment. He feels that he and his mother are one. This is called the "dual unity." There is no differentiation between the infant and the mother. As far as the child is concerned, what the mother experiences and what he experiences are the same thing. In the symbiotic stage, if there is anger, there is no difference between the baby feeling the anger and the mother feeling it. Gradually, as the child starts to separate, he becomes aware that there is another human being there and begins to experience himself as separate.

However, that early merged state, that state of being the same as the other, remains as the basis of projection. So when you feel angry, you may feel someone else is angry. The child is feeling angry, and he doesn't know his mother is different from him, so he thinks she is feeling angry, or vice versa. The reason it is so hard to see through projection is that in the merged state, the mind has not developed enough to be aware of what is happening. The mind and the personality have not yet developed. So when you are projecting, you are acting at the pre-verbal, pre-conscious level. Your mind isn't even involved in it; it just happens. That's why we take our experience to be reality—because we cannot distinguish what is inside from what is outside.

Besides forming the basis of projections—such as the superego projections we've just discussed—the merged state in the infant's symbiotic phase has another important aspect that we call "negative merging." When the child has negative experiences with the mother, the whole world is felt as negative. There's no separation between the infant and the mother, so in that merged state the whole world is anger, or the whole world is frustration, or the whole world is fear. The negative experiences with the mother gradually coalesce and become one big thing that is isolated from the positive part of experience. This forms the basis of the negative judgments of the superego. You project your superego outside because in the beginning, the outside and the inside were one thing. Now when you experience the negative merged state, you cannot separate what

is real inside from what is real outside, and your preference is to believe it's outside. So you can see that in order
to work through your superego, you must go all the way
down to that pre-verbal, chaotic, hellish, negative merged
state. And when you get down to that, you feel lost, you
don't know what is going on, there's no firm place to stand.
There are swamps wherever you turn—up, down, left,
right—all swamps. That's how you experience it; everything
is negative. As you experience this fully, without defending against it, certain essential states arise to move you
through this negativity and hell.

I've talked so far about how the basis for projection is
the merged state and the basis of the superego is the negative merged state. Of course, the merged state is not only
negative; there are also positive experiences with the mother
where the merging is fulfilling, satisfying, pleasurable, and
loving. But remember, it is still merged. There is no difference between you and your mother. So, for example, when
you are experiencing love for your mother, you assume your
mother is feeling love for you. What you experience is
love; the whole world is love. You think your mother is
loving you, but perhaps your mother is feeling empty, deficient, needy, and attached. As a child, you are not intro-
spective; you only see what you experience.

So just as the negative merged state is the basis for the
projection of negative aspects of ourselves, the positive
merged state forms a basis for our projection of the positive aspects of ourselves. And what is that but our essence?
The negative merged state is the basis of our personality.
It *is* our personality. The positive merged state is our essence.
Because of the "dual unity" that happens in infancy, we
associate our essence—along with all the positive qualities
of love, value, fulfillment, satisfaction—with the merged
state, the positive merging with another. That starts the big
search, the search for the perfect merged state with the good

mother who will give you love, value, approval, pleasure, satisfaction.

So we see that we not only project our superego outside, we also project our essence. We tend to see what is best in us, outside. That doesn't happen all the time, but it usually happens when you are in love. If you remember times when you were in love, you'll recall that the other person seemed all loving, shining, wonderful. Right? Then after a few months, you wonder where the loving, shining wonderfulness disappeared to. You think it must be that he stopped loving you. But no, those qualities were an illusion to start with. It was a projection of your own essence. This doesn't mean your partner doesn't have essence of his own, but that wasn't what you were seeing. You were projecting your essence onto him. That was what you were really in love with!

Why do people fall in love? People fall in love because as they begin to expand, they start to get close to their essence. Then the unconscious, the personality, gets in the way. It is threatened by getting close to Essence. So you project your essence outside onto someone else and fall in love with it. What this means is that you still cannot tolerate your own expansion. If you think back to when you fell in love, it was at the height of a time of feeling good, of expansion. Suddenly, the right person shows up, and you're in love. You might have known the person for five years, but you had never seen him as wonderful. Suddenly he's acquired all this wonderfulness; all these suns are shining through him! Look at his eyes! Don't you see that sweetness? Don't you see the stars inside? Why didn't you ever see this before? "I just never saw him for who he really was," you say. What's actually happening is that you are seeing yourself for who you really are. It is true that when you are expanded, you tend to see the other person's essence more. But that flash, that sudden perception of wonderfulness, is your projection of the same thing in you. You have it, but you think he has it. That's basically what happens when you fall in love.

Positive projection happens when you start becoming more and more aware of your true nature, your essence. Before this, what you know best is your personality, and that's what you project. When you start to experience your value, your love, your essential self, your compassion, all kinds of issues arise from the unconscious, barriers against experiencing Essence. This will make you want to project it outside.

This has been happening with many of you here. It's the same process as falling in love, except that now the expansion is coming from intentional work. As you expand, you see, love, and admire particular qualities in other people that often are not really there. This causes you not to see them in yourself. You are not willing to own them as yours; in fact, you are attempting to give them away.

In this group now, some people are experiencing a regression to the positive merged state with mother that existed at a very early pre-verbal stage. In the merged state, the child doesn't know that the wonderful thing she is experiencing is not the mother but herself. Mothers generally love their children and express their love now and then (if the child is lucky). But most mothers, as far as I can tell, are not really in contact with their own essence, at least not in a consistent way. As a person starts getting deeper into herself, regressing to those earlier stages, she gets to the deep layer of the unconscious that has the merged state imprinted on it, that very early symbiotic state where the mother had all the good qualities. So the positive projection may feel wonderful and sound like a good thing, but it's still projection, and it still lacks objectivity.

Projection, displacing something onto an object or seeing something that doesn't exist, is obviously for the purpose of defense. There are generally three levels or three varieties of projection in relation to the merged state, depending on the depth at which you're operating, or at which the unconscious is functioning. The first level is that of the actual merged state where you can't tell whether it's you or somebody else; you experience one big unity that is all wonderful. That comes when the merged state itself is activated. The other person might be participating or not. In the merged state, it doesn't matter. The other person might be sitting there, not feeling anything, while you are full of merging and believe that the other person is experiencing the same thing. That is the most fundamental, the deepest, level.

The second level comes a little bit later with more differentiation and separation. Instead of being completely merged, you project an aspect of yourself, such as value, onto somebody else. You see that value in someone else, and you want to merge with it. You project it and then you identify with it. This is the basis of what is called *projective identification*. This happens for negative affects too. You can project your fears onto someone else, then identify with the person and be afraid and share the person's fears. This is the basis for a lot of what happens when you admire someone or have an idol or ideal person in your life. You idealize someone and then bathe in their sunlight. The sunlight is actually yours, but it's hard for you to say that it's yours, so you say, "Oh, here's the sunlight; let me bathe in it. It's wonderful!" Another form of projective identification involves projecting feelings and then unconsciously manipulating the other so they actually feel what you are projecting.

The third level is just projection. You don't identify with the projection; you just project. "This person is very angry with me. It has nothing to do with me; it's all his own anger." You do this whether what is projected is something you want or don't want.

So depending on what level you're operating from, you could be just projecting, in projective identification, or in the merged state. There could be negative affect, positive affect, or Essence. Projection or projective identification of Essence becomes one of the primary barriers to owning and integrating your essence. You keep thinking that you don't have it fully, that you can't have it unless you are with someone else, or that someone has more of it than you do. I know people who are actually very fulfilled, but they continue to believe that it's because someone loves them. Or they continue to think somebody else has it. They say, "I want to be like them. I'll be happy if I just get a little bit of it," when they've already got it! They're actually throwing away their essence, hoping to get mother, to get the merged state.

It's a very tricky business. The reason it's tricky is that the perception of Essence can come very close to the perception of certain emotional states. As many of you know, Essence is not an emotional state; it's not an emotion. Essence is *being*. It is something that is actually, substantially there. Most of you fail to understand the significance of this point, so you tend to confuse Essence with emotional states.

When we experience Essence, we tend not to value it as much as it deserves. We do this for many reasons. One reason particular to this Work is that it is easy to get. In a year or two of working here, you start experiencing your essence which, throughout history, has been purported to be very, very difficult to achieve. So when you get it in this easier way, you tend not to value it. The culture we live in is materialistic. The more you pay, the better the thing is that you bought. If you get something without paying a lot, you don't think it's worth much. It works the same way with your true nature. Because it is easy to get, a lot of the time you don't see the significance or the value of it. You don't realize that without Essence there is nothing; without Essence there is only suffering.

That's why sometimes I think we should change the whole thing. "Maybe I should let them work for ten years, then I'll talk about Essence. Maybe then they'll value it." That is the method used in the past. In the old times, a teacher let his students grovel for ten years, working very hard, one disappointment after another, until their egos were totally ground into the dirt, totally gone. Only then would they have experiences of Essence. Then perhaps our students would say, "How wonderful! It's the best thing that ever happened to me! I did all this hard work for ten years; I really paid for it, and now I can enjoy it."

There is another, more universal, reason why you don't value your essence. We talk about how much your suffering resulted from the lack of love in your environment. Your environment wasn't supportive, wasn't loving, did not respond to you according to your needs, did not see your value. This is true. But we don't see the fundamental thing that happened. The fundamental thing that happened, and the greatest calamity, was not that there was no love or support. The greater calamity, which was caused by that first calamity, is that you lost connection to your essence. That is much more important than whether your mother or father loved you. You lost your own love because of that. Because your value wasn't seen, wasn't responded to, you lost your connection with your own value. Because your joy was responded to with hostility or judgment or disapproval, you had to cut it off, and you lost it. Now you believe you will have it only if you get approval. You think you will have value if somebody sees the value in you.

Why should you care whether someone else approves or not? If your essence is going to depend on the approval or perception of other people, then it is not free. We look at what happened in childhood so we can see how we lost our essence and how we can retrieve it. If we continue believing that we have to get what we didn't get from the outside, we will continue to do what we have done all our lives! And this is what causes our misery and suffering. Because our environment wasn't hospitable, compassionate, loving, or supportive, we think we can get satisfaction by getting an environment that is loving, compassionate, perceptive, and appreciative of who we are. What we are saying is that we want that positive merging again, otherwise we're not going to feel good. "I have to have somebody who loves me. I have to have somebody who sees me, who values me." It is true that this is useful and supportive at the beginning, but if you continue depending on it, this will stop you from owning and being who you are. Being who you are, being your essence, should be completely independent of any other factor, inner or outer. As I said in the beginning, Essence is the life. Essence is the fulfillment. It's not the environment, not the situation, not the job. It is Essence itself, your essence.

There is another reason why when we start perceiving our essence, we start seeing it in other places where it doesn't exist and tend to idealize and admire situations or people who don't have what we believe they have. The reason is that when our essence is lost in childhood, when our parents didn't see our value, didn't value us for just being there, our own value was lost. The essential aspect of pure, absolute value is gone. A deficiency results, leaving a hole in the place of that loss. When an essential state is cut off, the result is what we call a hole, a deficiency, a lack. We attempt to fill that hole by trying to get value from the outside, instead of seeing that the value was ours to start with and that we were just cut off from it.

But there is an even more difficult complication, which is that one way to fill the hole is to make a false value, to pretend you have value when you don't feel that you really do. It's too painful to feel the absence of value, so most people create false essence to cover up that feeling of lack.

This is what the personality consists of—false qualities of Essence. We call the personality the "false pearl." Each person retains the memory of what was lost and will try to imitate it, try to act, believe, and feel in ways that are so close to the essential states that after a while the person fools herself and other people as well. Some people do this more than others, and some people are better at it than others. The personality is really nothing but an impostor trying to take the place of Essence. These false qualities of Essence—what we call the crystallization of personality— are what we see in most of the people around us who are considered successful. Everyone else believes they've got it made. They appear to have genuine qualities of confidence, compassion, self-assurance, and self-esteem but, for the most part, these are false qualities. Just as these people have convinced themselves that these false qualities are real, they convince almost everyone else as well.

As we begin to get in touch with our own essential states again, we tend to be innocent and naive. For instance, when we begin to feel our own value and we come upon false value in the world, we tend to believe real value is there. When we begin to experience love and see false merging love in other people, we tend to think, "That person's got it too. Isn't that wonderful!" This is when objective perception is needed to see what is actually there, especially since we have all kinds of unconscious reasons to want to believe the other person has it, the situation has it, a certain group has it, or a particular ideology has it. It is so hard for us to feel that we ourselves actually have it.

We think, "If I'm the only one who's got it, I'll end up all alone." Yes, you might end up alone. Alone and happy. This doesn't necessarily mean that you will *have* to be alone, but it does mean that you have to make the choice of being *willing* to be alone, if that's what it takes to own your essence. Eventually, you will be faced with this choice.

Do you want to be "loved," "appreciated," "seen," and be miserable, or do you want to be "alone," "uncared for," and happy, genuinely happy? That's a choice everyone will have to make. That is the true independence. The true realization is that your essence is not dependent on your exterior life at all. The whole world might be against you, but if you are your essential self, you will be content.

What we're doing here is fundamental. We're not playing a game of getting a little something here, a little something there. There's no real resolution, no real fulfillment until a person is totally committed to the Work and can face being alone. Essence is the answer. You have to see and accept that completely. Nothing else will do. No half measures. You have to go all the way. Absolutely all the way. When you start realizing what your essence is about, it doesn't even matter if you are threatened with death. Who cares? Live, die—what's the difference? If other people don't like you, it's fine. It's all the same to you. You're not going to change yourself to suit anyone else's ideas of how you should be. In fact, you can't have real intimacy until you can tolerate your own aloneness, integrity, individuality. That is freedom.

As long as you hold onto wanting something from the outside, you'll be dissatisfied, because there's a part of you that you are still not totally owning. How can you be complete and fulfilled when there's a part of you that you are not owning? How can you be complete and fulfilled if you believe that you can't own this part until the right conditions arise? If it's conditional, it's not totally yours.

So to recapitulate, we need objective perception to understand that Essence is the answer, Essence is the fulfillment, Essence is the Ridhwan. And from that will result the true value of Essence in yourself, in others, everywhere. Then, with that understanding and valuing, there will arise the true discipline, the true protection for Essence and for the essential life. The world we live in does not support this.

People around us do not support this. There are pressures everywhere against this orientation. When you experience Essence, it needs to be protected. You have to find your own citadel, your own fortress. Your citadel has to do with the true discipline; it *is* the true discipline. There is an actual aspect of Essence that we call the citadel, which is the protection for your essence so that it will be preserved and develop and can be used for others. This is the right way of living. It has to be there. It's not that you'll experience your essence and automatically get out of the swamps. You have to take action, to live your life in accordance with the truth, the truth of your essence, the truth of who you are, your situation, what your limitations are. These need to be taken into consideration in the way you live your life. It's not going to just happen—there are too many external forces against it. It is your responsibility to protect and guard and preserve your essence, your true nature. You couldn't do that as a child because you were totally dependent, but now you have the chance to preserve and protect your essence as you experience it.

How do you find the true discipline? How do you find your citadel? Essentially, true discipline means using will in the service of truth. It is the merging of will and truth. It means that the will of Essence is in service of the truth of Essence. It means you don't use your will in the service of personality. This might vary from one person to another. No one can tell you, "You should wake up at five o'clock in the morning, meditate for two hours, drive to work by yourself, read a book about such-and-such during your lunch hour." You have to find out by yourself what to do. You find your truth and use whatever will you've got to live according to that. It's not just going to happen. You have to take the responsibility to actualize the truth.

You need to use your truth, and you need to use your will in harmony with the truth. For that to happen, the will needs to be objective, and the truth needs to be objective. Objective, as I said before, means not influenced by your emotional state or your unconscious. You need to use your objective will in the service of objective truth. Using your will in the service of objective truth means using the objective will of Essence according to the objective truth about how things are—not according to your emotions, not according to your beliefs, not according to your dreams. It has nothing to do with desires or preferences. It has to do with how things are, how they function. That's what "objective" means: to live according to the facts, the truth. As long as you say, "I want it another way," you are going to suffer.

To be even more efficient, both will and truth must be not only objective, but universal as well. "Universal" in this case means not only the truth about you, but the truth about the whole situation, about everything and everybody. Also the will is not only for you but for Essence as a whole. You will see that for you to really live the life of Essence, the life that will protect and nourish and nurture Essence, you have to take into consideration everything and everybody. It has to be universal. When the will and the truth are in harmony and both are objective and universal, that will be the citadel. It will protect the sweet, soft, fulfilling Ridhwan. Ridhwan is sometimes called the "Angel Guardian of Paradise." It is subtle, soft, and delicate.

What I said today is something everybody is going to have to struggle with. That's just the way it is. The only thing you can do is alter your perception of who you are, which means becoming free of your personality.

TEN

The Value of Struggling

I want to make clear the value of a certain aspect of the Work. Sometimes we forget it or don't realize its value. What I have in mind is what we call "the struggle"— struggling with oneself. The usual orientation of people who want to work on themselves is that they want somebody to take the struggle away and give them something easier. The end result of this would be what Gurdjieff called the "stupid saint." Another name for it is the "happy vege-table." If you want to be a happy vegetable, you can find someone to take away your struggle and make everything easy for you. Many people here unconsciously act out a desire to be "saved" by a teacher. But if a teacher "saved" you, you would lose something. You would lose the value of struggle.

One manifestation of the failure to understand the value of struggle is those students who come to me whenever they notice something is amiss in their lives. They think they should ask me about it. They don't think about it for themselves; they don't persevere. Instead, they come and ask me about it. "I have this problem in my life. What should I do?" What you should do is work on it on your own. You need to do all you can on your own to work with the issue, really struggle with it, deal with it, experience it, see everything you can about it. When you've done everything you can about the issue, when you've struggled with it so much that your mind can no longer do anything about it, then you can bring that burning issue here. Then you can ask the question.

So there are two ways to approach the teacher. One approach is to hope the teacher will take away your problems; the other is to use the teacher, not with the expectation that she will take away your problems or offer solutions or "make it better," but that she will give you a little push in your struggle.

If you haven't really struggled with a question, you cannot digest the answer even if it is handed to you. The struggling is the same thing as the process of digestion. It's easy to come up with an issue. It's relatively easy for me to see what it is about and how to resolve it. But you yourself must have your personal perception in order for the resolution to be a true resolution. I could say this or that and you might go home happy, but the resolution would not be embodied. It can't be yours; you can't see it. If you do not embody something, it is like being blind.

You might go very far in this direction, every day finding an issue and saying, "Oh good! Another one! I'll go ask AH about it!" You'd come to me, and I could be so nice. I'd show you this and that, and you'd get an answer or some sort of insight. But after a while, you'd need me the way you used to need your mother for milk. You wouldn't be able to do without me. The result would not be an embodiment of realization but a complete dependence. The end result is a happy vegetable that needs someone to water it every day. If it isn't watered, it starts shriveling up.

Even though your struggle seems very painful and difficult at times, it has its usefulness. It is an integral aspect of working on yourself. The struggle is, in a sense, a process of internal combustion. You could, of course, be a stupid saint or a happy vegetable if that's all you want. But then you would miss out on being a genuine adult, a mature human being.

I'm not here to take away the problems and give you something yummy. I'm not here to save you from your problems. I'm here to show you how to struggle with your problems and resolve your issues. I'm here to show you how to make wine, how to grow the grapes and take care of them, how to press them, how to work with them until they turn into wine. You need to learn how to make wine for yourself. If I do it for you, you'll have to keep buying wine. But if you use me in a way to learn how to make the wine yourself, then you will become an adult, which is what this Work is really about—becoming mature human beings who do not need or even want to be fed or watered by someone else.

Many people see their situation from the perspective that they have problems and they have to get rid of the problems. But this is not the way we work here. There is something that needs to be done, and it can be done through a certain process. Part of that process is the struggle. You can see your struggle as a struggle with problems, or you can see the struggle itself as a problem (although it isn't really that way). The process is about allowing your mind to accept conflicts and difficulties. In the end, the struggle with the personality will bring out Essence. It cannot be done in any other way.

People sometimes complain, "How come it's so difficult? Why do I have so much trouble, so much pain?" It's because you're not looking at things from the right perspective. It's true that you have pain. You see it as bad. But it is bad only if you think the whole thing is a problem. If you look at it from the perspective that this is a situation to learn from, then it is simply a chemical reaction. In a chemical laboratory, you have all kinds of things: many different substances, Bunsen burners, instruments that are used for the processes of heating, evaporation, condensation, and coagulation. You could say, "I really don't like this heating up part of the process. I'm going to get rid of it." But if you get rid of it, how can you have a chemical reaction? Can you imagine having a chemical laboratory without fire in it? Without heat, nothing would happen.

I would be cruel and uncompassionate to take your struggle away from you. And you would be doing a disservice to yourself to get rid of your struggle. You need to see this from the correct perspective and get involved in it, embrace it. In that way, you are making yourself. You are actually working to make yourself. And the deepest realizations, the most genuine satisfactions, the most lasting fulfillments are those which are personal to you, which are very intimate to your heart. They are your own. They don't really have to do with me or anybody else. Your deepest inner struggle and the substances, the juices, that come out of the struggle are of utmost value to you. Nobody else can do that for you. Struggle is the salt of the process. Without it, your life would be bland. Your achievements would be bland. You would not be able to value them. Without the salt, without the struggle, they would not be rooted in you, and you would not be able to embody them.

Struggle is a friction inside you. That friction will make certain parts of you get sweeter and sweeter. I'm not talking about indulging in suffering. I'm not talking about causing pain for yourself. I'm talking about genuinely grappling with whatever situation is at hand, taking responsibility and really confronting it, whatever it is, and being there for whatever issues, whatever problems, whatever conflicts, whatever situations you have in your life. Completely embrace them; involve yourself wholeheartedly in life. Do your best to observe and experience what is happening and to understand it. When you are in the struggle, you are involved with yourself. You can know every little part of you, definitively.

So, a central value of the struggle is that it helps you know yourself. But it has other ramifications as well. One of them is that to struggle and grapple with an issue completely and wholeheartedly is the way to develop your belly center, your Kath. It is the way to ground your realization, your attainments. Then you will be like a tree with a very deep root system—strong, healthy, with deep roots that nourish it continually. A tree with shallow, weak roots can produce pretty and tasty fruit, but a wind can topple it.

Also, your struggle in the Work is a genuine, total response to the deepest longings and yearnings of your heart. It is an acknowledgment of those deepest longings. Without struggle, you have to dismiss those yearnings for the deepest aspects of you and of your reality, and you will lead a life that is superficial, a life without depth, without roots that reach deeply into your true being. The more you struggle with an issue, the deeper you will be as a human being. If your problems are taken from you or if you discharge them quickly without really exploring and understanding them, you will deny yourself the opportunity of reaching more deeply into your being.

The same is true with essential states. You might experience a sense of your own value by working through a certain issue, but that is not the end of it. The experience of value, the value itself, can get deeper if you struggle with the issues even more. The effect becomes more concentrated. It's like apricot juice—if you simmer it, it will begin to evaporate and get thicker. On the surface, where the juice is turning to steam, it seems lighter, but below the surface, it is getting thicker and denser. It is the same with Essence—lighter on the surface, denser underneath, and getting thicker and more concentrated the more it simmers, the more heat there is, the more you struggle.

Of course, it is very hard work to struggle with the issues of your life. But that work is what differentiates a baby essence from an adult essence. The value a baby embodies is something like amber, a light amber essence. Mature value is like a deep, thick, dark amber. There is no maturity without struggle. If you remain on the level of a baby, satisfied with a tit that provides, you continue to be a baby. You don't grow up. A baby eventually grows into an adult by confronting his life and learning about himself through the process of struggling with the difficulties that are part of his life.

When you have an issue in your life, the point is not to get rid of it; the point is to grow with it. The point is not just to resolve the issue; the point is to grow through resolving it. So, in many ways, you can see that maturity has to do with this growth, this broadening, this depth.

In terms of actually doing the Work, what does this mean? I said earlier that struggle is the salt of the process. It is not insignificant that the personality can actually taste salty. When you are working on issues that have to do with the personality, you might actually taste the saltiness. When you experience Essence, the taste is sweet. Personality is the salt, and struggling with the personality is what will bring you in touch with Essence, with the sweetness.

In terms of working here, the question you bring to your teacher has to be a burning question. If you have a feeling one day and don't understand it, don't run to your teacher saying, "I was walking down the street, and this person said such-and-such to me and I felt scared. Why was I feeling scared?" That is not a burning question.

Respect your issues, grapple with them, struggle with them. When an issue comes up, involve yourself in it, observe, pay attention, be present, understand it as best you can, using all the capacities you've got. Then, if the issue is hard for you to understand and you can't get through it and the fire is burning inside you, come and ask the question. It is that question which is the best question to ask a teacher. It is the right use of the teacher. When you ask that question, deal with it, and come to understand it, you will undergo a transformation that is not possible otherwise. Then you can take the realization and digest it, absorb it. But if you tell me to give you the enzyme and you haven't digested anything on your own, how are you going to absorb it? It's like trying to absorb big lumps that haven't been thoroughly chewed. No matter how much enzyme we put in, you'll probably only get a stomach ache.

The teacher is not really to be used for dealing with issues that you know how to work with on your own. The teacher is there to help you get to another level of the Work, to give you a push toward a different way of working, a deeper way of understanding yourself. If you are already on a certain level of understanding, a certain level of Work, you can use that understanding. When you use those capacities, the knowledge you use is making its own heat. It is creating heat on the level you are on now. You use that heat to try to understand what you're dealing with until you have exhausted yourself, exhausted your knowledge, exhausted your mind, exhausted your understanding. Then you bring the burning question that you cannot answer to the teacher. The answer will take you to the next level, a level you have not experienced yet. But you must first exhaust all your capacities at the level you are on, and then you will see there's something more. If you really get to that point, it means you are getting close to the next level. That's the real use of the teacher. Then the combination of the teacher and a little insight catapults you to a different place.

You can use the teacher to do your struggling, or you can do it yourself. Why waste your precious time with a teacher? Why waste the precious time of the teacher? The teacher can be put to better use. Your own struggle with your issues, doing your part to untangle your personality, will make the Work most effective. Perceiving your deficiencies, not defending against the hole and acting out your defenses, but seeing what you are identified with and allowing what is arising in you in that moment will create the friction that melts away impurities until what remains is what is true in you. As you continue this effort, a new capacity and maturity results. When you take responsibility for yourself, when you really confront and embrace yourself, you have life. That is the reality of what you've got. It is what you live. It is what you taste. It is what you smell. It is what you touch. It is reality.

The problematic situations in your life are not chance or haphazard. They are specifically yours, designed specifically for you by a part of you that loves you more than anything else. The part of you that loves you more than anything else has created roadblocks to lead you to yourself. Without something pricking you in the side, saying, "Look here! This way!" you are not going to go the right direction. The part of you that designed this loves you so much that it doesn't want you to lose the chance. It will go to extreme measures to wake you up, and it will make you suffer greatly if you don't listen. What else can it do? That is its purpose. How much suffering and difficulty it brings you is immaterial in relation to the fulfillment and satisfaction you will have when you actually struggle and see the fruits of the struggle. You can look at your problems as difficulties to be gotten rid of as fast as possible with the least struggle, or you can look at them from the perspective of the part of you that is guiding you to yourself. If you look at them from that more accurate, more finely tuned perspective, the new issues that then arise have a new value. They have nutrition that you need.

The whole process works with the utmost purity, the most complete intelligence and compassion. The most difficult things that happen to you are, on the deepest level, the most compassionate. Ultimately, the struggle with yourself leads to what is called the "Black Death," which is the death of the personality, when you wrestle it to the ground, struggling with it. That doesn't mean fighting, punching, kicking, screaming. Struggling and wrestling is the process of understanding. It requires persistence and steadfastness. You wrestle with it until it finally says "I give up." Ultimately, you reach the final understanding of the personality. When you see through to its source, its center—which is the experience called "Black Death"—you will recognize that the heart of this death is pure compassion.

ELEVEN

Truth

I want to take a popular expression, one everyone has heard but few understand, and explore it. The expression is "The truth will set you free." Why do people say that? People also say "Seek after truth" and call themselves "seekers after truth." People idealize being honest, sincere, truthful. Why? What's so wonderful about being truthful? Who said that being truthful is good? Well, I'm sure your mommy said so. Right? And they told you so at school. They told you not to lie. But why should that set you free? A lot of the time, telling the truth gets people into trouble. So what is this preoccupation with truth, truthfulness, honesty, sincerity? Where did all that come from?

We want to find out whether it's true that the truth will set you free. You've heard it for years, and you've believed it. It may appear that you still believe it, but you don't really. If you really believed that the truth would set you free, it would have done so. If you really believed it, you would have sought after truth every second of your life as intensely as possible. You would have found it, and you would be free. So, clearly you don't really believe that the truth will set you free, though you might pay lip service to the idea.

I think that from the perspective of our Work, the best way to say it is not, "The truth will set you free," but to say, "The truth will set the truth free." That is true: The truth will set the truth free. But what's the big deal? What does that have to do with us? The truth will become free. So what? What do we get from that? Let's look into this matter by investigating what truth is. To understand what we mean by truth, we have to look at what we mean by honesty, sincerity, facts, and truthfulness.

What does it mean when we say, "The truth will set you free"? What does it mean when I say, "The truth will set the truth free"?

S: The whole statement from Jesus is "You shall know the truth, and the truth shall set you free."

AH: Let's look at this statement and see whether that's true. "You shall know the truth, and the truth will set you free." How can that be? Let's take the statement "Today is Sunday." Is that true? Yes. Does that set you free? Here is another example: Today is Sunday, I am a male Caucasian, my hair is dark, I'm wearing a blue shirt, and I am sitting here talking to you, investigating truth." Does that set me free?

I saw one of those soap operas on television a few nights ago, and in it one person said to the other, "Why don't you tell me the truth?" The other replied, "That's not the truth. Those are the facts; the facts and the truth are not the same thing." She was right; the facts and the truth are not necessarily the same thing. It is a fact that today is Sunday. It is a fact that I'm talking to you now. It is a fact that we're investigating the truth. It's a fact that it's morning and it's cloudy. Are these facts the same thing as the truth that will set you free? If they are not, then what is the truth that will set you free?

Now let's take the words "honest" and "truthful." Usually, when we say we're being honest, we mean that we're not lying. I'm being honest with you, so I'm telling you the truth. There's also being honest with yourself, not lying to yourself. So honesty is generally taken to mean that one is not lying. Let's go a little deeper. When we are talking to someone, we can tell them the facts or we can tell them everything. Suppose you know a certain fact about yourself, and you feel that to be truthful is to communicate that fact to another person exactly the way it is. Will telling this truth set you free?

Suppose you're in Nazi Germany in 1940, the time when they're hunting Jews. You hear a knock at the door. Your Jewish friend appears and says, "Will you hide me?" He is your friend, and you know he will suffer if discovered, perhaps be put in a concentration camp. So you hide him. Later, someone else knocks on your door, very loud. "Who is it?" you ask. "The Gestapo." You open the door, and the Gestapo officer asks, "Is such-and-such a person here?" Now, what's the truth? Is it being honest and truthful to tell him, "Well, yes, as a matter of fact he is here and he's hiding in my cellar"? You're working on the truth, right? You're a seeker after truth; you believe that the truth will set you free. So what do you tell the Gestapo? Do you remember your spiritual practice and say, "I am truthful and honest, I can never lie, otherwise I can never be enlightened," and tell the Gestapo, "Yes, he is hiding in the cellar"? Would that be honest? I have exaggerated the example, but it makes the point.

Another example comes from something we talked about at our last meeting. Molly wants to talk to her sister about doing the Work, but when Molly talks about it, her sister becomes defensive and angry and doesn't want to listen. Molly knows that her sister acts like this because of the way she feels about her father and mother. Should Molly tell her, "You don't want to listen to what I am talking about because you're angry at Mom"? Would that be honest?

S: Yes, but it would be an attack.

AH: So what does it mean to be honest, then? We are seeing here that to be honest, the way we usually mean it, has its limitations. It does not take all the truth into consideration. It is a superego attitude, a moralistic attitude. "If you tell the truth, you're good; if you don't tell the truth, you're not good. If you tell the truth, you'll go to heaven; if you lie, you'll go to hell." We see that sometimes the rule you learned in school isn't true. We are learning that there is a bigger truth here than the fact that your friend is in the cellar. There's the bigger truth that the other person is from the Gestapo, that your friend is a Jew, that if the Gestapo gets him, they'll probably kill him. So which is honest— telling the truth or acting in a way that takes into consideration the larger truth, the truth of the whole situation? What is more truthful? In this example with the Gestapo, it is obvious.

We're seeing that acting according to the truth is bigger than giving a truthful answer when someone asks you a question. In the example of Molly talking to her sister, part of the truth is that Molly's sister is not able to hear certain things at the present time. If Molly tells her these things now, her sister will have an even harder time getting to the actual truth. So we see the truth is not just the facts, not just something you believe in. It is bigger. It is the whole situation. To be really truthful, in the broader sense of the word, is to take everything into consideration.

But we still have not really answered what truth is in the saying, "The truth will set you free." We can find a bit of

a clue by looking more closely at what we have just discovered—that you need to take the whole situation into
consideration. What you need to ask yourself is "Why?"
Why should Molly take the whole situation into consideration when she talks to her sister? What's the point?
What's Molly's motivation in talking to her sister? Is it just
to tell her the truth? Or does she want her sister to know
the truth so that the truth will set her free? And with your
Jewish friend, don't you want to act according to the whole
truth so that your friend will be free?

The truth is useful and important for one purpose: to set
you free. Let's go into this aspect of it. Why will the truth
set us free? Christ said so, but why is it true? That's our
real investigation. How can the truth set you free? As I said
at the beginning, it's more accurate to say that the truth
will set the truth free.

You could say, for instance, that by understanding yourself, knowing the truth about what you experience and the
reasons why, you will be free from those emotional reactions and conflicts. Right? You will be free from the things
that bother you and weigh you down, the things that make
you feel miserable. Isn't that how you think about it, that
the truth will set you free? You believe that the work on
self-understanding, seeking the truth, will set you free. Here,
we go beyond the superego position to knowing the truth
about yourself. We see that the more you know about yourself, the freer you are from your false personality. You have
more capacity to cope with your emotional reactions and
the situations in your life if you know the truth about them.

For instance, Molly's sister is angry at Molly and isn't
talking to her now. They are having a hard time with each
other. Now if Molly's sister found out that she's not talking to Molly because she's angry at her mother—she's not
angry at Molly at all—that perception by itself will direct
the anger at her mother and will free her from relating to

Molly as her mother. It will allow her to relate to Molly in a freer way so that their relationship will be more real. In that sense, the truth, if she saw it, could set her free from that reaction toward Molly.

We have seen in the Work here that the more you look at yourself, the more you understand the way you are now, how your personality has developed, what motivates it, and what keeps it in place—in other words, if you understand your fears, angers, and hurt, in time, this understanding will set you free from them. The reactions of your personality will not have the same power and tenacity as before. You'll experience more and more freedom and expansion. You'll be more free to feel yourself. You'll be more free in your actions and in your interactions with others. This is what the Work is about. "The truth will set you free." From everybody's experience here, it does work this way.

But if that is the case, you might as well go to New York, find yourself a good psychoanalyst, and work with her for several years five days a week. By the end of the analysis, you would be "free." You would find out the truth about your emotions, your conflicts, and so forth, and that would set you free, since according to what we've seen so far, understanding the truth about yourself will set you free. If this is the meaning of "You shall know the truth, and the truth will set you free," then all you need is a shrink. Some people, especially shrinks, believe so. We could go into an elaborate discussion with case histories and show that it isn't true that psychological knowledge ultimately sets people free. Knowing the psychological truth about yourself doesn't set you free. You arrive at a measure of truth, a measure of freedom, but that's it.

S: The whole quotation is "Seek the Kingdom of God, and you shall see the truth, and the truth shall set you free."

AH: Aha, I see. He said to seek the Kingdom of God.

S: Yes, and he said that the Kingdom of God is within.

AH: So obviously you can't go to a shrink for this. You might go to a priest; maybe that will help.

S: Maybe a priest and a shrink.

AH: So that's a good point: The truth has to do with the Kingdom of God. Maybe that's part of the additional information we have to take into consideration. You probably remember that when we talked about the Theory of Holes, we said that psychological difficulties and emotional problems are not due just to emotional conflicts, but rather the emotional conflicts are the result of being cut off from certain parts of ourselves, from our essence. That is a truth, too. It is another fact. I have this emotional difficulty, this problem, this conflict in my life, not only because I don't understand my emotional history, but because I am missing something—the Kingdom of God. We call it Essence, the true nature of ourselves.

So we see that to know the truth means much more than knowing yourself in a psychological or emotional way. Part of you has been cut off and is not available to you. If you have an essential experience and you've seen the connection between Essence and the loss of Essence, you can say, "Finally, I know what Christ meant, how the Kingdom of God fits in, how knowing the truth fits in, how the truth can set you free."

Now let's investigate what truth is from a slightly different perspective. This might add to our understanding that so far seems to be complete. The fact that it is Sunday is not exactly the same kind of fact as the fact that I am feeling sad. That today is Sunday is a convention that we have agreed upon. Probably in China, it is Monday already. Such facts depend on the place and the people and so on. So there are truths or facts that we know are facts because we agree on them. "I am sad" is not in the same category of truth. It is a subjective experience. It has less to do with a social contract or agreement. How do I know that "I am sad" is true? It's not a social convention. What if you don't agree? You might say, "You don't look sad to me." How do I know I'm sad and what this sadness is about? It can become quite complicated. You might say, "I'm sad because today I was rejected by my wife." You talked to your wife and she told you she was going to run away with someone else. How do you know that's why you are sad? How do you know you are sad because somebody did such-and-such?

Or you're sitting around and suddenly you become aware that you're feeling hurt. It is a deep hurt in your chest, like a wound. After a while, you say you're feeling hurt because you were abandoned by your mother when you were two years old. You seem to be certain about it. How do you know? It's not a social convention; nobody is there to corroborate this truth, and you seem to be certain. How do you know that it's true? Did you ever ask yourself that question? Can you prove that you're sad and hurt because your mother abandoned you when you were two years old? Where does that sense of certainty come from? After all, your mother is not right here abandoning you. It happened long ago. What makes you so certain now about what happened then?

When I ask you that, you answer that it feels true. I ask, "What do you mean—*it feels true*? How do you know?"

"That's what I feel," you say. "That's what I remember. It feels real."

If I'm a good objective scientist, I will ask, "Who says it's so? Are you saying that just because you say it feels true, it's true? What does this mean, telling me it feels true? When you say it's true, you seem to believe it."

"That's how I'm feeling."

Sometimes external consequences demonstrate the truth of your self-description. If you were sad when your wife left and cheered up when she returned, on that level at least, your understanding was accurate. If, in the earlier example, you connect your sadness with a sense of being abandoned and work out the issues about your mother, perhaps accepting a sense of aloneness or self-sufficiency, then again your understanding is corroborated.

But at the moment you were feeling it was true, what made you believe it? Was God sitting there saying, "This is the truth"? If we can find what gives our insights certainty, it might lead us to understand more of what it means to say, "The truth will set you free."

Let's take something even less precise, less verifiable, yet where the sense of truth, the sense of conviction, is stronger. Let's say you have a conviction about an insight. Maybe you're meditating, considering something, or working with somebody, and suddenly something pops up and *you know*. Suddenly there's an insight, a knowing. "Yes. That's it." It's direct, certain. I think everybody here knows the experience of insight because you've had many insights. "Aha! That's what it is!" When you have an "aha" do you question it? Do you ever say, "Wait a minute. There's an "aha," but let's try to prove it"? Why don't you question it? What makes you so certain it is the truth? In the moment of insight, your head feels expanded, something lets go in your body, and you say, "That's it." After a while, you may get all kinds of corroboration, perhaps a bigger picture that corroborates the truth of your insight. However, at the moment of the insight itself, there was no proof. What made you believe it?

Sometimes, a few minutes after the insight, another part of you might question; but at the moment the insight is there, the moment that explosion inside you happens, there really is no questioning. There is certainty. You know, if only for a split second, that your perception is true. You're so certain that the question of whether it is true or not is not even an issue. It is so. What is it in the insight that gives you that certainty, that conviction, that there is truth there?

I've been talking about an isolated insight. Suppose one day you're working with me and you get an insight. After three minutes you get another insight, and after two minutes another insight, and after one minute another insight, and after a half second another insight, and they just keep coming one after another in a continual expansion. It's possible to get insights one after another without losing that sense of certainty. You have that conviction, that certainty, flowing through you continuously. What is that? What's the thread that makes you certain? Don't you think there might be something in that experience of insight—a flavor, a taste, a feeling that makes you unquestioningly know it is true? Isn't it as if there's some part of you that is more present now than at other times? Maybe it is the voice of God telling you it is true. That's how Socrates knew. He had a voice always telling him that something was true or not true.

Let's try to identify what that thing is that gives you that conviction, that certainty, the something that makes an insight have more truth than just an ordinary perception. In the experience of insight, isn't there more of a sense of freedom than in ordinary perception? Don't you feel a sense of expansion, a lifting, a sense of satisfaction?

An insight generally has two things: the content of the insight and the energy present in the insight that gives you the sense of certainty and expansion. Insights will continually have different content, but the sense of expansion is consistent; it always has the same quality. You value insights because their content will set you free and because there is a sense of freedom already in the insight, much more so than in your day-to-day perception. So we see that insight contains something besides just the fact which we call the truth. There's actually something in the insight, the energy of the insight that gives the satisfaction, a certain joy, an expansion, a sense of freedom. Isn't that more of what we're looking for? Isn't that the kind of freedom that we want, that we suppose truth will give us, something that comes close to ourselves?

If it is true that the truth will set you free, why doesn't ordinary perception give that same kind of freedom? The same truth is there. The insight, "Oh, that's why I'm disappointed—there's no snow today!" could instead happen as a normal perception. "What a disappointing day—no skiing." Why does one perception have a sense of satisfaction and freedom and not the other? Why does insight carry more sense of certainty? It's the same fact, the same truth.

We're seeing something here about insight, that the truth is not just a matter of knowing a certain fact. With an insight, there is an energetic sense in your mind and body that indicates more certainty and gives you a sense of freedom that is more satisfactory. It's a more palpable, lived sense of freedom. As further insights occur, they go deeper, and the certainty also gets deeper. When this process continues for some time, you might feel there is something in the air, almost like a taste, a fragrance. You taste, sense, smell, and feel something almost sweet, satisfying. There is a sense of an intimate kind of closeness to yourself, along with a freedom of expansion. There's a sense of satisfaction that goes with the experience of insight. It is more than just: "I'm free from this." Every time you have a moment of insight, it's as if you open the perfume bottle for a second and close it again. It's as if you have smelled something—freedom, satisfaction, whatever. Having one insight after another is like opening the bottle many times. You can smell the aroma continuously.

So there is something in insight that allows us to know directly, without questioning, that something is true, more so than in the experience of ordinary perception. That sense of certainty seems to be intimately linked with the sense of satisfaction, a sense of being more intimate with oneself, closer to oneself. What does it mean to get more intimate and closer to yourself? There's more warmth, more satisfaction. There's a sense of freedom and truth. The facts have led us there, although the facts were not exactly what we were looking for. What we're looking for is that sense of intimacy, closeness, freedom, satisfaction.

Now we're seeing how knowing the truth will set you free. We're getting the taste of freedom, the taste of satisfaction. Knowing a fact will open up something in you and make it more available, but the facts themselves are not important. Every insight has a different fact in it—sometimes it's your mother or father, sometimes it's anger or hurt, sometimes happiness—these change. It is not the facts but the satisfaction that is the common element. Maybe the person who said, "The truth will set you free" knew this.

So you went out looking for the truth. You knew facts were truth, but what the person had in mind was that particular inner certainty, that taste. If you go after the facts, the true facts, these will bring you to the taste of that satisfaction and freedom. It is not a moralistic thing that truth is good, and you will be rewarded if you are truthful. The certainty that comes with truth is itself a freedom, the freedom from doubt.

Sometimes the fact itself might be extremely painful. The fact might be remembering that your father didn't really love you. But even in the pain of that, there is satisfaction because you know the truth. You're closer to yourself; you're more you. What gives you that sense of satisfaction is not the fact itself. We usually think that, given time, a fact will set us free and we won't have to react one way or another. But now we're seeing it from a more subtle perspective. If you follow the fact deeply, you'll get a taste, a sense, a satisfaction that is much more directly linked with seeing the truth than we first imagined when we heard the phrase, "The truth will set you free."

Perhaps if you go deeper into the insight, into the satisfaction, and follow that aroma, you will come to the bottle with the perfume. If you have the bottle, you will have the aroma all the time. You can open it whenever you want to and enjoy the fragrance. You seek the truth to find the perfume.

In moments of insight, what you're seeing is the truth. What allows you to know something is true is that truth is present. This sounds like a tautology—knowing the truth because truth is present. However, it is not exactly that. When truth is present, it is as if you are tasting something in your heart. There is a sense of satisfaction, a sense of warmth. That is the golden thread. That's the truth that makes a statement true and meaningful. That's what makes you know, "When I'm feeling this, I know I'm feeling this. I know I'm hurt because my mother abandoned me." It's not that somebody has logically proved it to you, but truth is there. There is a part of you that is truth. Looking at the facts will set free the part of you that is truth. That part of us is not the fact, has nothing to do with facts. It is what makes the fact true, and it is there regardless of what the facts are. The facts can change; they are always changing.

There is an absolute truth that makes relative truth true. You know that the relative truth—that I am disappointed because I lost my job, that I don't like the fact that there's no snow today—is true because there is a scent of absolute truth in it. It is what gives you the conviction, the certainty. When you follow the thread of absolute truth, you come to the whole truth, which is nothing but the truth of you. It is Essence. That's why you feel closer to yourself. That's why you feel more satisfaction, more intimate with yourself. So the truth will set you free.

There is a simple reason why seeing the truth, especially the truth about ourselves, leads us to this intimacy and satisfaction. We are generally kept apart from our true selves by false ideas about ourselves. Seeing the truth often involves seeing through these false ideas, allowing us to recognize the deeper reality which we are. Thus knowing the facts will free you from your emotional reactions, and being free from your emotional reactions will free that part of you that is truth. When you seek truth, you seek yourself. The truth will set you free by allowing you to be yourself.

In the search for truth, you have to start with reality. Reality is what is here at this particular moment. It's Sunday, and I'm talking to you. This is the reality. It is also the truth, but it is a certain aspect of the truth. If you feel loving as you listen to me talk about truth, that is the reality of you at this moment. The truth is more what makes you feel loving right now. It's not enough just to see that you feel loving; to get to the truth, you must see what makes you feel loving at this moment. This distinction between reality and truth is very important. We need to see the reality in order to proceed to truth. Reality is the fragrance of truth, the result of the truth. The relationship of reality to truth is like the relationship of gold dust to solid gold.

It is true that at any given time your state is colored by emotional things like certain deficiencies and certain losses of Essence. Maybe you say, "Okay, I'm going to work every second from now on so I can be free of my deficiencies." It's a fine wish. However, the reality of the situation is that you have certain limitations that must be considered. You have a body, a stomach, a nervous system, and to be able to survive long enough to find the truth, you need to eat, sleep, feel safe and comfortable. Because there are certain parts of you that are not available all the time, there's no point in pushing yourself and beating yourself up because you're not working on your deficiencies every second. You have to take your reality into consideration. Just as Molly needs to consider the reality of her sister, you need to consider your own reality when you work on yourself.

We have seen that the way to truth is through reality. Reality points to an aspect of the truth. Truth is more than reality, but reality is what we see at the beginning: Things are as they are. We need to see them as they are, not as we want them to be. We need to know exactly what's happening right now in the present situation. Knowing exactly how it is will automatically guide you deeper into the truth.

So, do you have an answer to the question, "What does it mean that the truth will set you free?" A half hour ago it seemed we had a complete understanding. Now you see that that understanding was not complete. You see that when you know the truth, it will set you free, but not as a result. When you know the truth, that is the freedom. You are the truth. You are the truth that transcends all the facts. Seeking the truth will set this truth free. The truth is the essence of your heart. It is the real metal of your heart, the gold of the alchemists. And it's the truth that doesn't depend on any statement. When you experience yourself as truth, there is no statement that is true. You just are truth. "I am the truth." When you are asked, "Who are you?" you reply, "I am the truth." That's why some of the Sufis call God "Al Haq." Haq is the Arabic word that means truth. One of the names of God—which means one of the aspects of Essence—is Truth. I think understanding it that way will help us to orient ourselves more toward the truth.

The truth is you. And without you, facts are irrelevant, useless. When you free truth, you free yourself. Truth is not just something that you use to free yourself; it is the essence of you. So we see a progression. First, we looked at truth as a moralistic thing. Then we saw it was utilitarian, that it is useful to find truth because it will lead us to freedom. Now we see it in a deeper sense. It's not that it's useful to find truth; the truth is you. It's not like truth is going to lead you to yourself; the truth is you. Truth is your very nature.

What does it mean when in the Sufi stories they say, "You'll be free when you love truth for its own sake"? It means to love yourself for no reason but because it's you. When you love the truth, you love yourself. Mohammed said, "Whosoever knoweth himself, knoweth his Lord." When you know truth, you know God.

People think, "Okay, now let's find out all about my emotions. How come every time my boyfriend comes home, I am glad to see him and want to be near him, but I act really cold? I should try to find that out." That's not what Mohammed meant when he said "Whosoever knoweth himself..." He didn't mean that. To know yourself is to know the truth. And truth is Essence. Of course, to know the facts is the way to reach the truth because the facts have truth in them, little atoms of truth. If you know a lot of facts, you have a lot of those atoms, perhaps enough to make a big nugget of truth. The point is not to collect the facts. The point is to make that nugget more clear to us. The deeper the facts, the more truth is in them, and the closer they are to who you are. The deeper you go, the more you will experience the truth in them, until you reach a point where there are no more facts, just Truth.

TWELVE

Allowing

I n our Work, we do not seek the harmonious life by putting Band-Aids over our difficulties or patching up the rough spots in our personalities. Regardless of how useful we find the results of therapeutic techniques, we see them as bandages for little rips here and there. That is fine for therapy, but it is not the Work. I think most of you know by now that everything in you is connected with everything else in you and that Band-Aid therapy does not reach deeply enough. We are concerned here with growth, transformation, and development, not with therapeutic intervention or the results of therapeutic techniques.

This Work is, however, therapeutic. It has therapeutic results in the sense that change occurs and conflicts are resolved. Yet doing therapy is not our orientation; it is not what we are primarily interested in. What is most important is to facilitate the growth of a human being.

To be able to cooperate with transformation rather than oppose it, we need to understand what characterizes any process of growth. What is the most characteristic thing about the process of growth that differentiates it from other processes?

S: It involves an expansion.

S: There is always something changing.

AH: Let's look at it a little more closely. What does change mean? What does expansion mean? It's true that growth involves change. What does change require?

S: Awareness.

AH: Yes, an expansion of awareness. Awareness is required. But that does not explain what change is.

S: Letting go, a release of something.

AH: Okay. That's a way of seeing it. That's part of change. What else?

S: It requires some kind of action.

AH: But what does change mean? What does growth mean?

S: Transformation.

AH: Yes. But what does that mean? We want the definition of transformation, of growth, of change. If you look in the dictionary, how will change be defined?

S: The presence of something that wasn't there before.

AH: Which requires what?

S: Letting go of the old for something new to develop.

AH: Exactly. That's what the process of change and growth and transformation is. That is the literal meaning. If you get out the dictionary, it says that something will become something else. If, by definition, transformation means a change of something into something else, what we start with is not what we end up with. What we end up with might be completely different.

We need to look at this more closely to understand what this implies. To explore this, we will look at the hopes and aspirations you have when you first start the process of inner growth. You come here with certain beliefs and aspirations of what you want to happen. You come here saying, "I want to be free from my fear. I want to be happy. I want to have a better job, more lovers, a better car, be more objective." Right? That's what's on the agenda. Everybody comes wanting something. Some people have vague ideas; some are more definite.

But what does transformation mean? Doesn't transformation mean that even these aims will change? Your aims belong to who you are now, and if you really change, you will change into somebody else, and that new person might not have the same aims and aspirations. If you hold onto those same aims and aspirations, those same ideas and plans, you'll continue being the same person. There will be no change. There will be no transformation, no expansion, no development.

If you want to grow, you have to be willing to actually be somebody with different thoughts, ideas, beliefs, and experiences. You come here saying, "I want to be happy." Fine, you want to be happy. But it might be that to be happy, you will have to become a different person. Maybe the person you are at the present time is an unhappy person. You say, "I want to stay the way I am, but I want to be happy." Well, maybe that's not possible. Maybe part of the character of this person you are now is unhappy. Maybe you're made of unhappiness. How can you be the same person and be happy? To be happy, you have to be a different kind of creature.

Everybody has all kinds of ideas about who they are, how things should be, and what makes a good life. If you want to change, you have to be willing to allow these old ideas and beliefs to die. If you say, "I want to grow and still be the same stubborn person," there is a contradiction. How can you change and still be the same?

The essence of transformation can be seen in the process of change that results in a butterfly. There are several stages. One of them is a larva; the larva eventually develops and becomes a butterfly. So when you first come, you're a larva—small, big, yellow, black, African, European—it doesn't matter. You say, "I want to grow," and in your mind, growing means becoming a bigger, happier, more colorful larva. Isn't that how it goes? You don't think, "I'm going to be something totally different." You don't want to be something totally different. You want to be a bigger, more beautiful, more loving larva. It never occurs to you to be something other than a larva. The concept of butterfly never enters your head. It's not even in the realm of possibilities.

So you see, there's a problem here. If the larva continues to be a larva as it grows, it will feel constricted after a while. It's getting bigger, it's growing, but there is something definitely wrong. It complains and goes to a therapist. The therapist will help it change a little here and a little there. "No, don't eat those maple leaves. They will make your indigestion worse." It tries one doctor after another. It goes to a chiropractor to get its spine straightened. It goes to a masseuse so it will relax. But it never occurs to the larva that it's not going to feel better as long as it continues to be a larva.

That's how everybody actually thinks. Nobody thinks: "I'm a larva who's going to be something else, something that I have no idea about now, and I can't even think or say what this might be." A larva can only think of larvae. A larva doesn't think of butterflies. It sees butterflies and thinks, "What interesting creatures. Where could they have come from?"

We all have our preconceptions, our set of beliefs about change. Maybe you believe that if you grow, you'll be more intelligent and have fewer problems and make more money and your stomach won't hurt as much. Or maybe you believe that growth and change means you'll be married and have two children and two cats. And it will be perfect if you and your husband each have a dog. So you start working on yourself and, after a while, you see that having all those things might not be what growth is really about. So you say, "Okay, one cat, not two. I can manage with just one cat. One cat, two dogs, a husband and two children." And, of course, a house someplace in the country and two vacations a year and continuous love from a few specified people. If you work on yourself for a while, you might be willing to let go of the two dogs. If you are seriously engaged in the Work, you might eventually come to feel the love and security within your own essence, viewing the external goodies as desirable but not necessary to your contentment.

There are many kinds of larvae. For your particular larva, changing might mean accepting two cats and a dog but no house in the country. Or you might find that two cats and one dog won't do, and you believe that for you to change, you need to have three birds. Or instead of a husband or wife, you might need to have five lovers at a time. These are just examples of how we approach the wish for change with fixed ideas about what change means.

Perhaps as a child you were interested in machines, and you eventually graduate from college with a degree in mechanical engineering and work as an engineer. But maybe after a number of years working as an engineer, you need to become something else in order to grow. Maybe the best thing for you is to be a gardener. Instead you say, "No, I have to grow and change and be a mechanical engineer at the same time. And I won't let go of any of my cats. I'm going to continue to be a mechanical engineer with my two cats and my dog, my house, and everything else. Otherwise, I'm not interested."

So, we're seeing here that the most elementary require-
ment for growth is the willingness to let go of what you
believe will make you happy. Because when you do change,
you are no longer the person who thought you knew what
you would change into. You will be a different person. The
needs of a larva are not the same as the needs of the butterfly it turns into. Maybe a larva needs two cats and a dog,
and a butterfly does not.

So there is a need for an attitude of allowing, allowing
things to emerge, to change, to transform, without antici-
pating how this should happen. You can direct things only
according to the way you are now. You can conceive of the
future only according to the blueprints you already know.
But real change means that the blueprint will change.

The only thing you can do is to be open and allow things
to happen, allow the butterfly to emerge out of the larva
and be a different being. You might be amazed, saying, "All
this time I thought I had to crawl faster! I didn't know it
was possible to fly." It is possible to fly, but if you just want
to remain a larva, you can learn to crawl a little faster. You
can even learn to crawl sideways. But it will never occur
to you that you can fly. You see things flying around you,
but don't think of flying because you haven't got wings. If
you allow things to happen, you might find that you do
have wings and you are flying around.

Usually the particular things you want and the ways you
want to experience yourself are determined by your self-
image. Regardless of what the image is that you want for
yourself, what it really means—if you look at it closely—is
that you want particular things because they will give you
certain inner sensations, feelings, or perceptions. You're not
really in touch with the cat; you're in touch with your inner
sensations. The cat makes you feel a certain way, and that's
what you really want. You don't want a cat because it's a
cat. You want a cat because it makes you feel a certain way

about yourself. What's the big deal about having a cat or a house or a husband or wife? If you didn't have a particular feeling about these, what difference would it make if you had them or not? If you felt the same either way, then why bother? You might as well have a rhinoceros.

So we are looking at this from the perspective of the inner experience. In the beginning, you want certain inner stimuli, certain sensations and feelings. At first, you may think that you want a house, a dog and a cat, a particular job, and so forth, so that you can feel a certain way—probably secure or comfortable or fulfilled. As a larva, you want certain inner stimulation and assurances that you see as a kind of nourishment.

But, as we have seen, to allow transformation, you need to be open to the possibility that even in terms of inner stimuli and sensation, what you want will change. The kinds of pleasure you valued so much before will not necessarily be relevant to the butterfly. It's a different stage. The pleasure of the child is not the same as the pleasure of a teenager, and the pleasure of a teenager is not the same as the pleasure of an adult. Often people say, "No, I want to have the same things. I want a tit, regardless of my age." But if you want a tit all the time, you continue being a baby. You just learn to hide what you want better.

You need to be willing to allow the quality and type of those desirable inner sensations and inner stimuli to change to something that you've never known, that you've never even thought about, and that you might not recognize until it happens. You might try to hold onto an idea that you want love and happiness, but maybe the love and happiness you want are not the same love and happiness that a butterfly would feel. Maybe the love and happiness of a butterfly are totally different from your ideas about it now.

If you continue to insist that you want the happiness a larva has, what will happen after a while? You might burst.

Something might go wrong. You might get cancer. The larva might start having a stomach ulcer, brain tumor, all kinds of things, because it's supposed to change. The larva may insist, "NO! I'm not going to change. I just want to be more loving in the ways I know." But when you begin to grow, you might find out that you don't feel loving, that you experience other kinds of sensations and inner stimuli. There might be something that feels like a breeze. But if you're not willing to allow yourself to have the inner sensation of being a breeze, you'll just continue feeling the same way, regardless of how much you work on yourself.

To try to restrict your experience is to be like a tree that says, "No, let's just have leaves. No fruit." When the fruit comes, you pinch it off or put masking tape over it. What will happen to the tree after a while? It's not only that it won't bear any fruit; something will happen to the roots and leaves because the tree is supposed to have fruit. You might say, "No fruits, only flowers. When fruit appears, stop them. Stop the whole show." So you get all kinds of chemicals to apply so that the flowers won't become fruit, because you've decided what's supposed to happen and what's not supposed to happen. Or you decide that the most wonderful thing is to have orange flowers, and that's it. If they're pink, you want to cut the tree down.

To have the quality of openness is to let something that you are not directing come out and emerge by itself. You're not saying, "No, what's next is a pomegranate." How can you know? If you're a tree, you don't know what's going to come out of you. A human being can predict that a pomegranate will appear on a pomegranate tree, but the tree itself doesn't know that. Let's say that after a while you see that you just want love; that's what you really want. But love as you know it is an emotional thing, an emotional kind of excitement or high. To let yourself change, maybe you have to experience love as a drop of honey inside your heart.

You may say, "No, there's no such thing as honey in the heart. Bees make honey. I use it on my toast, on my granola." You don't allow yourself something else: the possibility that at the next stage of development, your heart is full of honey. If you don't allow that, you'll never experience the deeper, finer quality of love.

So, you need to be willing not only to allow your dreams and your self-image to change completely, you also need to allow your inner experience, your inner sensations, to change in kind and in quality. Otherwise you'll stop your growth. After a long process of growth, you will discover that some of the deepest and most cherished inner sensations you can have are sensations or experiences of being yourself, the experience of your true identity or Essence.

A larva doesn't even consider such things. "There is no such thing as sensing myself. There is only going bowling and having a nice date. What does it mean to be myself? There is no such thing." When you allow for broader possibilities, you start appreciating different kinds of experiences where you can be more of who you really are, more intimate with yourself.

So, what you value will change. If you keep valuing the same thing, you won't change. You may discover that one of the most satisfying and fulfilling experiences is to feel your inner identity, to say, "That's me!" You shift from being concerned with external self-image to an inner recognition of yourself. You might even discover your essence. "Oh, that's me! Now I know!" You're all excited and that's great. But why stop there? It's not one discovery and that's it. How do you know? Maybe that will change too. Maybe it's not always going to be honey. Today it's honey; tomorrow it might be apricots. Now you think you understand: Essence will be sweet like something to eat.

That might be true, but you are limiting your experience again. If you allow yourself to have the attitude of allowing, of openness to the process of growth, you might wake up one morning and find out you're a planet! Now, you could not have directed your growth from an apricot to a planet. If you continued with the consciousness of an apricot, you could never even think of being a planet. You have to have complete allowing and openness for something like that to happen. Yet even at this stage, your mind can set limits: "Okay, now I see how the process goes: It goes from emotions to fruits to planets. Venus can be next, then Mars and Pluto." But you didn't know emotions could become apricots, and apricots could become planets, so how can you know it should stay planets?

Now you're getting smart: "I'm getting the idea. It's about getting bigger. Maybe the next thing I'll be is a star." So, you work on becoming a star. But the next thing that's possible for you might not be a star. You don't know. Yet every day you meditate and visualize a star. If you were open and allowing, you might discover that the next thing is not to become a star. You might find out, for instance, that the planet has things inside of it. The next step was not to get from a planet to Venus or Mars or even the sun, but to go inside the planet. And when you go inside the planet, everything might go *poof!* and disappear. And there will be no emotion, no apricots, no stars or planets—just nothing, complete nothingness.

This sort of experience reflects the freeing and development of various states and qualities of Essence by working through the psychological issues associated with them. Because the content of the unconscious issues is, by definition, unknown to our conscious minds, and because the different levels of Essence are not only unknown but unimaginable to the personality, having expectations or preferences about what will happen next can only interfere with the process of freeing our essence.

The process of essential development has its own logic, which you can discover only as it happens. You might find out that if you allow yourself to be nothing, suddenly that nothing becomes a different something. So you're no longer the planets, or the apricots, or the stars; you're a totally different universe. You might find that you are a certain kind of planet that becomes a different kind of planet, and the planet is made out of diamonds. It's not a planet we know anything about. Suddenly everything is diamonds; even the trees are made out of diamonds. You look at the people and they don't look like people; they look like shiny eggs walking around. Now, how would you know that from the beginning?

I'm not saying these particular things will happen. I'm trying to eliminate the ideas and barriers in your mind to allow for possibilities that you cannot conceive of. There is no way for you to conceive of these things as long as you are set in a particular place. To allow the process of growth, you need to allow that anything is possible. Anything can happen. You don't know what it will be. There is no way for you to know the next step. If you try to direct it in any way, you're just going to stop it. You can only be yourself, be what you are now, and allow the next moment to unfold. After all, the core of life is a mystery.

What I'm doing is opening your mind so you can allow and perceive a certain attitude, a certain way of being. The freest attitude for the process of growth is the attitude of complete allowing. You are not passive, and you are not active. You are allowing. We will see that the process unfolds from one thing to the next. The process emerges if you give it the space to emerge. Your most important work is to understand the barriers you have against the unfolding. Wherever you are, you look at yourself and understand what your barriers are, what the things are that are stopping you from fully experiencing what is there. When you do experience fully, you don't try to hold on to the experience or determine what direction it will take. You just experience it fully and that's it. Your mind is open for anything to happen.

This requires a certain trust in the process, a trust that there is such a thing as transformation, and that it will be good, that it will be the best thing. The attitude of trusting without knowing what will happen, of allowing things to emerge, is needed at all levels and stages of the process of inner development. It applies to the external level, the emotional level, the subtle levels, essential levels, all of them. Any idea of how things are going to be will only work as a boundary. The moment you have an idea of how things should be, you're creating walls and sitting inside them. There is no trust in yourself, there is no trust in reality, and there is no trust in the process of transformation and growth. What is there is restriction, and you'll suffer and complain as usual. When we allow the natural process of growth, there is expansion, happiness, and joy.

Joy is simply the freedom of the process of transformation. You allow yourself to just be, and change, and grow, wherever your being takes you. This process has joy and happiness in it. The moment you try to restrict it or guide it in a certain way, the joy will close, and there will be heaviness, sadness, and pain. Also, trying to predetermine where you're going is uncompassionate and shows ignorance. How do you know what is going to come next? How do you know what your life is supposed to be like? How do you know what you're supposed to feel inside? You can only trust it to happen.

Let's say you have a certain experience of your essence. You feel truth. You know you embody truth, and you feel full and wonderful. Your openness has allowed this to happen. Soon you might find yourself with an attitude that says, "I want to feel like this all the time. I don't want to lose this. Now that I have my essence, I have to keep it. I'll fight against my personality." Or you might rationalize your wish to hold on to the state of truth by saying, "I have to keep this because I'm usually deceived by lies, and staying in this state of truth means I will be a better and more honest person." All this is true. But the state of truth may only last a few seconds, and your attitude toward this must be open-ended and allowing. Something else might take its place. If there is the slightest holding or attachment of wanting to keep it, you are erecting a boundary, a wall.

It's a matter of a small perspective and a large perspective. Working towards goals or certain changes is useful a lot of the time, but it is a smaller perspective than simply allowing things to happen.

S: Working towards something doesn't mean you're creating boundaries?

AH: Sometimes you are creating boundaries, and it's useful to do that for a while. But you need to understand that you're doing it for a while, for a certain purpose, and that it is not the largest perspective. When you're working towards something, you shouldn't forget that it is a small perspective and there is a larger one. And even when you're working towards something, you need the attitude that anything can happen. You're working towards something, but the experience itself needs to be open and completely spontaneous.

Allowing is not passivity, and is not an act of determination. It is neither of these. It is between passive and active. In a sense, you're actively being passive to your experience.

Are there any questions?

S: In my job I feel like I'm sort of floating around and I'm not happy with what I'm doing. I wonder if I should try this or that. When do you start being active and pursue something else, and when should you just float around? Is it a matter of when the urge gets strong enough, you'll do it and not worry about it, or what?

AH: What I'm talking about doesn't mean that whatever you feel like doing, you go ahead and do. A certain attitude is required, an attitude of allowing what is there to be there. For you, allowing the reality might mean allowing yourself to feel the dissatisfaction and see what it is you really want, see what the situation is. The point is to not make limits. You're asking me to give you a rule that you can use, a rule about being active or passive, but what I'm saying is that there are no rules.

S: Where does the trust come from?

AH: You allow yourself to be open. Usually, when you feel you don't know what's next, you want to do something right away. But you don't have to do anything; you just need to be there. When something happens, you're there for it. Ultimately, trusting is really trusting your essence. That will develop; the trust is not something you have right away. The more you know yourself and the more you see the rightness of your own process as it unfolds, the more you'll trust it.

At the beginning, you will knock your head against the wall many, many times, trying to push this way or that way. In time, you'll learn that the best thing is just to let it be, to allow. Part of the process is developing this trust. As you observe this more, you'll see from experience that every time you try to set your experience to go a certain way, there will be frustration and pain. And every time you see how you're limiting yourself, it will bring freedom and expansion. When you see that many, many times, the trust will develop more. When you really trust, you will see that your essence will always emerge, your true nature will always come through, and always in better ways than you could have anticipated.

You have had some experiences like that, and they will increase. Finally, you see that there is nothing you can trust—nobody, no authority—except the process itself. Finally, the trust is not trusting a person, not trusting a theory, not trusting any authority; it is trusting reality. It is just trust, confidence in Essence itself. It will take time for trust to mature and deepen.

You will tend to trust in certain areas and not in others. When we have more fear, we tend not to trust. We stick to our walls more. But when you find out over and over again that it is fear, more than anything else, that makes you hang onto your walls, you will tend to let go of more of the walls. The more free from fear you become, the more willing you are to let go of those walls.

Part of the process of development and growth is learning to trust the attitude of allowing. The final development is not trying to have your essence in a particular state, but allowing whatever is there to happen. So, the final development of allowing everything to happen is nothing but the final dissolution of the personality, because the walls are the personality. They are made by the personality and fueled by the personality. The personality is nothing but these boundaries. So to take this attitude means not taking the side of the personality. It is not even taking the side of Essence. It is not taking sides, not having prejudice. The process of development is a continuous unfolding, very intricate, very vulnerable. It goes up and down, in and out, sideways, all directions, all ways. That allowing quality is the very freedom you seek.

This allowing position is an alternative that your mind doesn't usually see. Your mind can see that there is this way and that way, but there might be hundreds of other ways. Which way is broader, more expansive—to be free while your environment is the way it is now or to be free only when it changes? The perspective of allowing is to see that these are walls that can be removed. The perspective of allowing is so big that it can see the walls and allow them to be there. It is so big that it transcends even the issue of whether there are walls or not. Either way, you allow. There can be an open space in the middle of a wall. So allowing

can enable you to tolerate stuckness when you are working through a belief or feeling and identifying with it. The
whole process of dealing with an issue happens within the
space or attitude of allowing. Allowing has no restriction.
It is the greatest freedom. It is a freedom that does not say
it wants to be free from anything. It is a freedom that is just
freedom, whether there is a wall or no wall.

So from one perspective, all you see at first are walls.
From another perspective, you see that light can get through
the cracks. And then there is the broader allowing which
is to see from the beginning that there are no cracks or walls
or any of that. It is all the same. You are not restricted by
restrictions. Restrictions appear the same as openness.
How can you be restricted by them? This is very different
from the way the personality thinks. Personality thinks that
it has to be this way or that way for me to be free. "I have
to remove this wall in order to be free." And that is true
in the beginning because removing the walls is removing
the personality. However, the final wall that needs to be
removed is the belief that there are walls, that there is a
personality that needs to be dissolved. Then you are free.

When you understand the space of allowing completely,
when you understand that walls and openness are the same
thing, then even freedom loses its meaning. You're free from
freedom. You don't say, "I'll be free." You don't say, "I am
free." You're free from that.

You see, it's a subtle thing. The moment you say, "There
is something that needs to be removed," there's already a
predisposition, already a direction. It is a restriction. The
moment you say, "I want to remove this restriction," you're
creating a restriction because you're saying, "I want it this
way and not that way." Who does that but the personality?

This is not something to make into rules of conduct. What
I'm saying here is to open your mind. To know freedom,
you need a certain perception, a certain attitude that will

itself bring freedom. If you're thinking, "I know what to do about that situation," you're not allowing. Allowing is a state of being. It has nothing to do with "I'm going to do this or that." It's an attitude—a final attitude—which is the absence of any attitude, or the allowing of any attitude. You allow even not allowing. Otherwise you're making a restriction.

The moment you take any stance, you are putting a wall in the allowing space. Even when the stance is allowing everything, the only thing you can do is just live your life completely. The mind does not know what to say. What is left is the purest nature of the mind itself: complete allowingness. The freedom is so free that it allows boundaries. I'm sure each one of you is stuck in a certain boundary someplace as I'm talking. Each of you can recognize the restrictions of your own world that you're dealing with right now. Do you want to keep it the way it is or get rid of it? As long as there's a part of you that wants to go somewhere or finds another part unacceptable, there is no freedom.

THIRTEEN

Growing Up

I consider our work situation a kind of school. One important distinguishing feature of a school is that it is not a nursery. I think if we try to understand the differences between a nursery and a school, we might understand better what it is we're doing here. The main difference is that a nursery is for very little children, and a school is not. If you go to a school and believe it's a nursery, you probably won't learn anything. You'll just be a pain in the butt for the teachers. "Isn't this a place to be taken care of, given things, made to feel safe, protected, loved and all of that?"

In a nursery, the small child is not expected to take care of himself. An adult takes care of the children. An adult provides for, protects, and watches over the child, and the child is not expected to be responsible for himself. In a school, a child is expected to have more responsibility. In fact, that is one of the things a person is expected to learn in school—to have more responsibility for his own learning. The teacher gives you information and direction, and you go learn by yourself. You do your homework at home; the teacher doesn't do everything for you. Of course, students might complain about the teacher. They might complain about having to learn math or chemistry, but those are the subjects that are taught in school. Whether you like it or not is not the problem of the teacher or the school. If you decide to go to school, then these are the things you have to learn.

In this school, we have the opportunity to grow up. It is a school to grow up in. In society at large, the usual situation is like a nursery full of little children. The main difference between an actual nursery and society at large is that a nursery is recognized as a nursery while society at large believes that everyone is an adult even though everybody is still a child pretending to be an adult. In a nursery, a child doesn't pretend he is an adult. Our Work is to learn what it is really like to be an adult, to find out what growing up is really about. Because of that, we can't treat people like children here, or they'll never grow up.

All the problems you have exist, quite simply, because you don't want to grow up. You don't want to behave like a grown-up; you want to continue being a little baby. The fact that you don't want to grow up, that you want to continue being a baby, explains almost everything you feel. It explains, for instance, the common pattern of people being angry at the teacher for not doing or being enough for them. They say, "Why don't you do more for me? Why is it so difficult?" What they're really saying is "You're not a good mommy!" This is exactly how babies feel when mother is not being what they want. An adult does not think that way.

An adult looks at the situation and asks, "What is the best way this situation can be used? What can I get out of it?"

There is no place for complaints in this Work. What do complaints do? Complaints are used only to keep Mommy around. You complain to Mommy, and Mommy makes you feel better. When you are an adult, what's the point in complaining? If you feel angry at your teacher or at the schedule or the parking situation, you are thinking that Mommy should be there to take care of you, to fix the situation. But you're supposed to be learning to be adults, which means to do the best you can do in the situation. You do not come here to be given something. You come here to grow up.

The same pattern happens in every part of your life. When you are in a situation where something doesn't go right, most of the time you get angry, you complain, you get sad about it, you blame the other person, or you blame yourself. What good does that do? Do you see that only a child would behave that way? If something doesn't go right, an adult will look at the situation, see what she can do, and forget about the rest. Everything else is just a waste.

I'm not putting you down. That's not the point. I understand why most people behave like infants. Our purpose here is to become aware of what is actually happening, to see that most of the time we act like children, and our difficulties arise because we want to continue being children instead of growing up. You might believe it is wonderful to live the life of a child, to play and have no responsibilities, but if you look at the child, it's not really that enviable. A child is dependent; a child has no freedom. She has no choices. The life of a child is very restricted. The adult is different. An adult has freedom; an adult has choices. So you can't want to continue to be a child and then complain about things not being your way, because children don't have things their way. If you want to have things your way, you have to grow up and make them your way.

Let's look more closely at the process we're engaged in here. We're saying that this Work is basically a process of learning to grow up. It is not a matter of getting *better* or becoming a more perfect person. It is a matter of growing up, with all that growing up requires. A neurotic human being is a childish human being. A psychotic human being is an infantile human being. A healthy human being is an adult.

What is the difference between a child and an adult? The most important feature is that the baby is unable to feed and protect himself. The parents do these things for the child. Then the child grows up and does these things for himself and for his children. An adult is a person who can do these things for himself and does not expect somebody else to do it for him. An adult is one who is aware of the situation as it is, sees what is there, knows his capacities and limitations, and acts accordingly. An adult is realistic and knows what to expect from a situation and what not to expect. Instead of acting according to his unconscious beliefs, an adult sees what a situation actually provides and what it does not.

For example, believing that your partner will give you something—love or security or self esteem—is the belief of a child, because it is obvious, if you look clearly, that the person will not or cannot give you such things. When you are acting like a child, you continue to believe that the other person is supposed to give you certain things. When she doesn't, you get angry and blame her. If you were an adult, you would have known from the beginning what the person was capable of. But usually we don't see the person for who they really are. What you unconsciously believe is that this person is your mother, and you continue feeling and behaving like a child towards her mother—expecting things and being angry and disappointed when you don't get what you want. An adult does not do this. If something doesn't happen, she says, "Oh, I see. I'll do it." But when a baby wants something and the mother doesn't come, the baby cries and makes a fuss. That's what most people do with their friends, right?

When you relate to another human being, you aren't really relating to another human being. Instead, you are constantly relating to that person as if he or she were your father or your mother. The main reason you continue relating to other people as father or mother is that you want to continue being a baby. You want to look at other people as if they were adults and you were a child.

This becomes clear if you look at how you feel most of the time. You feel that everybody else is an adult and you are sort of a kid. So you expect certain things, you're angry when you don't like something, you want things to be your way. You see mommies and daddies everywhere, and you hope you'll get what you want if you are just good. This applies to how you feel about the Work. You feel that maybe if you do this Work, you'll be lovable and wonderful, not like you were when you were a little kid. You hope that finally, Mommy and Daddy will find out you're really a lovable kid and will take care of you. They'll comfort you whenever you want it, and every time you want a lollipop, someone will hand you one to suck on. That is one of the main reasons people come to the Work. They think it's the way to be a successful kid. "How nice it would be," they think, "to understand more and expand more so people will think I'm wonderful and want to be around me and do things for me and give me what I want." Our unconsciousness, our inability to see things as they are, is mainly because we don't want to grow up. Our unconsciousness is the unconsciousness of a child. It is nothing but continuing to see things the way you saw them when you were about a year old.

To become aware, to become conscious, means to grow up. It means seeing things as they are. When you see things as they are, you'll see there are certain things you need to do. There are certain things you can get from external reality, and there are things you can't get. There are basic laws about how the universe works, and an adult is one who is aware of these basic laws and acts accordingly, not like a child protesting and complaining. When rain falls, it falls downward. You can make a fuss about it falling downward if you want it to fall upward, but no matter how much you cry about it, it won't fall upward.

A person who has not grown up will unconsciously see other people—men or women—as walking tits. Most of you see people as a mass of tits coming toward you or going away from you. You wonder: "Are they big or small? Do they have something inside them? Will I get it or not? Will that milk suit me or give me a stomach ache?" Isn't that how we look at people? Or we worry: "Is this tit going to be too big, too much milk? Will I drown or suffocate?" What complicates the situation is that the other people are looking at you the same way. So it's like two tits checking each other out, each of them trying to find out where the nipple is.

In a sense, what is generally called "the life of an adult" is really just a second babyhood. When we are children, the functions of nourishment, care, protection, release of tension, and comfort are provided by the parents—particularly by the mother when the child is an infant. As the personality of the child develops, the child becomes more independent of the mother, but this is accomplished by introjecting the mother, recreating her inside. You have your mother inside you and so, in a sense, you are still a baby. You still have your mother around, and you believe you need her. That is why, when you go deep inside yourself in the Work, you start realizing how much you want your mother, how much you don't want to lose her, how much you fear separation, all of that. Deep inside, you still believe that you need Mother around.

The mother inside you is not a physical thing; you have her emotionally in your unconscious. You behave like her, and you seek out people like her. You feel the way she felt, or you find people who treat you the way she treated you. In these ways, you always have Mother around. The ego or the personality of an adult is really a baby, except that now the mother is in a different form. Even those who deny they want mother, who had a negative experience of mother, continue to unconsciously seek the negative mother while consciously feeling the opposite. The mother is still pretty much the same mother you had before. You project that image outside and want other people to be like her, or you look for other people to perform those mothering functions for you, or you look to society for security, or comfort, or sustenance.

So emotionally, the personality continues to have a symbiotic relationship with mother. We grow up physically, but not emotionally. We continue to unconsciously believe we are dependent in ways that an adult human being doesn't actually have to be. You see yourself as dependent on others for love, approval, recognition, support, nourishment, contact, pleasure. Most people think that's the way it is. They think, "How can you be a grown up person and have a career and a good life unless you have a mate or at least a lover?" That's how most people think. They don't question it. They think they need love, and it is true—they do. But what they are seeing is the personality. The ego functions through emotional dependency, and you call it love.

Even when you are by yourself, not married or in a relationship or in a group, you are still relating to your mother—the mother inside you. You relate to your superego which is always beating you up. Why is your superego beating you up? Because it makes you feel that your mother is around. When you were a child, your mother was always judging you. So every time you feel like a little kid, your internal mother comes and beats you up. Then you feel secure. You might complain, but you feel secure.

School—a regular school—helps you to become an adult in some practical ways. You learn how to remember information. You learn skills that can help you to earn a living. You learn to do what your teachers teach you to do. But school does not teach you to grow up psychologically. In this school, we allow you the opportunity to grow up psychologically, to become an adult on an emotional level, to become really autonomous. You learn how to provide emotional sustenance for yourself. You learn how to give yourself love, compassion, approval, recognition, support, and strength. You stop believing you need those things from the outside.

Most people complain, protest, and feel miserable when they don't get love from the outside. An adult does not complain; an emotionally grown up person has his own love available inside him. He no longer has the unconscious belief that he will die without love from outside. You might think from this that growing up means to be alone, isolated, unable to relate. But that is also the fear of a child. Only a kid would believe, "Oh, I'll be all alone, by myself. That's really scary!" An adult isn't scared of aloneness or loneliness. An adult knows that he has a choice about being alone or being with others.

What essentially happens in the process of really growing up is that you don't need your mother or your father any more. You don't need to have your mother inside you or outside you. In the course of dissolving the mother inside you, you have to deal with the fear that there will be nothing there to support, protect, comfort, or nourish you. You must learn that you have these capacities in yourself. What takes the place of the mother—first the physical and then the psychological mother—is your essence. To recognize, realize, integrate, and develop your essence is to become an adult. Your essence is you. It is not something you learn from your mother. It is not being like her or relating to your superego. It is being your real self. Then you will have what your mother gave you in your physical babyhood: love, compassion, support, intelligence, consciousness, protection, pleasure, fulfillment, release—all these things. Essence can give you these things because Essence is support, is strength, is intelligence, and so on.

If you look to others for these things, you will get exactly what's there. And what is that? Psychological babyhood. Essentially, everybody is deficient and hungry, psychologically poor, weak, unconscious. What you get from the outside is frustration, suffering, pain, and disappointment. Only if you turn to Essence will you find real love, support, consciousness, intelligence, strength, and protection. That is where they exist in a pure way. It is a basic and obvious truth that if you turn toward the outside world, you will get the pain that prevails there, and if you turn toward Essence, you will find those things you want. You will find your own essence, which is the source of all the things you thought you wanted from the outside. So the process of growing up is learning that basic law and learning how to turn towards it more and more until you are completely, totally, the very nature of your essence, seeing that it is all there, all that you need.

This is the reason all disciplines, past and present, and all religions talk about looking inward. "Look inside yourself," they say. "Know yourself." It is not a moral or religious law; it's just how things are. It is not that you will be good if you look inside; it is just the only way it will work. It is the most practical thing. I have talked about this many times. When I talked about the heart latifa, I said that the main thing is the orientation of turning inward or outward. If you turn outward, not only will you get what is outside, but by the very movement toward the outside, the inside will close. So if you turn outward, the heart closes. If you turn inward, toward your essence, it will open. This is the basic law of the heart.

This principle is formulated in different ways. There are two main ways of working with it. One is the theistic approach, and the other is the nontheistic approach. The theistic formulation has been the main approach in the West. The Judeo-Christian and Moslem traditions were formulated around the existence of a deity or God. These traditions say that if you look toward God, you'll go to heaven, and if you look toward anything else, you'll go to hell. What is needed is complete faith, complete surrender, complete openness, complete turning toward God. This is nothing but the movement toward Essence, for God is nothing but the nature of Essence, the essence of Essence, the source of Essence. So if you turn toward Essence, the source of Essence, the nature of Essence, you will get the realm of the heart which is heaven. If you turn toward anything else, you will get what we call the "false pearl," the personality, and all the suffering and misery which is hell.

The nontheistic traditions—the Buddhists and Taoists, for instance—do not postulate the existence of God. The Buddhists speak of the Four Noble Truths. The first Noble Truth is that there is suffering. That is the nature of the personality. The second Noble Truth is that the cause of suffering is desire. The third Noble Truth is that there is a way out of that. And the fourth Noble Truth is the path. So there is suffering; its cause is desire; it is possible to have a cessation of desire; and there is a path towards that cessation. Desire here is the looking outward: "I want this. I want that. Give me love. Give me pleasure." It is seeking things from the external. The cessation of desire is the movement inward.

The theistic approach comes from the perspective of the heart. The other approach, the Buddhist one, is the perspective of the mind. They are basically the same thing.

Growing up is learning this fundamental truth, accepting it, and acting accordingly. You can cry and blame other people for not giving you what you want, but if you persist in the Work, you will finally see that's how it is. Along the way, you will protest. You will resist in many ways, gross and subtle, direct and indirect. In the process of growing up, you will have many fears about giving up the child's attitude because you believe that you don't have the capacity to provide what you need for yourself. You believe unconsciously that there is no other way but to look outside.

Yet it is possible to grow up. What does "grown-up" mean? You think of a grown-up as a person who can take care of you. Why don't you think you can take care of yourself? You believe your mother or father could to it; why don't you believe you can do it? The reason you don't is that you want to continue being a little baby and have your mother or your father inside you. When you are finally willing to grow up, Essence becomes your mother and your father.

In this process of growing up, you have to see through your pretensions of being an adult. When you see through those pretensions, you have to confront the facts of your childish psychological make-up. You have to see, experience, confront, and understand your smallness, your deficiency, your fears, your inadequacies, and what you believe are your inadequacies. These beliefs about your inadequacies and deficiencies are the basis of the feeling that what you have is not enough.

If you sometimes feel frustrated and disappointed because I'm not being Mommy and Daddy, that is something to be understood. If I were to play the role of your mommy and daddy, you would continue to be a baby. The purpose here is not to get Mommy and Daddy to take care of you or to make you feel better. In this school, we are learning to be adults, to take care of ourselves.

FOURTEEN

The Student's Relationship to the Teaching

I will say a few things today about your relationship to the Work, to the teaching, and to the person of the teacher. The Work has existed in many forms and many times, according to the needs of each culture. In a basic, fundamental way, the teaching is your lifeline. It is the lifeline to your real existence. That is a fact whether you like it or don't like it, whether you approve or disapprove, whether it makes you feel good or feel bad. It remains the truth. Your job is rarely, if ever, to accept or reject this fact, to prove it or disprove it. Your job, if you are sincere, is to try to see the truth about it, and how to utilize it to gain your real life. Without teaching, the ordinary person will remain undeveloped and will be only a potential human being. If you want to remain a normal human being, only

176

a seed of your own potential, you do not need the Work. But if you want to actualize yourself, to live as a human being, then you must put effort into seeing how the Work is the lifeline for real life.

The Work is not an addition to everything else you do in your life. If you consider it an addition, you will not benefit from it. The channel of influence, the channel of nourishment, will be closed to you. You must have the correct relationship to the Work for it to benefit you. If you take it to be something extra that you're doing, a little addition, something that is interesting, then it will be like everything else of little importance—like joining a club or signing up for a dance class.

For thousands of years it has been recognized that an individual who is connected to any system of the Work should make the Work the most important thing in his life. Otherwise it will not be beneficial, and it would be better that the individual not attempt to do the Work.

Most people do not like to hear this. They might have all kinds of thoughts and opinions about the Work, but they don't want to see this fundamental fact. It is frightening because acknowledging the true importance of the Work threatens your whole life. It threatens the false life by leading you to your real life. The Work is the lifeline to your real life because the Work is actually the lifeline to your essence, your being, your true nature. Not only is the Work the lifeline to your essence, the Work and your essence cannot be separated. So your relationship to the Work, to the teaching, must be the same as your relationship to your essence because the teaching and Essence are the same as the Work.

If you observe yourself closely, you will see that your relationship to the teaching is always the same as your relationship to your essence at that time. Often people will look at their relationship to the teaching from the perspective of authority. Whether they like to be "followers," or resist being "followers," they want to deal with the teacher as an authority. They must, therefore, go through all their judgments and emotional issues about authority. But it is not a question of authority here, of somebody who knows and somebody who doesn't know, nor a matter of following somebody else. All these issues are irrelevant when it comes to realizing the existence of your essence, to being real and actually existing as a human being. What do you care if you are being followed or you are following? It doesn't matter whether you are told to do something you like or you don't like, whether what is being asked of you is scary or not, whether you approve or disapprove. All these reactions are little things—small, irrelevant things when it comes to your real life, your humanness. To be Essence, to be your true nature, is actually to *be*, to exist. As I see it, the person who does not live as Essence actually doesn't live, doesn't *exist* in the fundamental sense of the word. The life of a person who doesn't know Essence, doesn't live Essence, is a waste really. I think many of you know this on some level.

What could help us in this work is a basic way of looking at things that will help us understand the particulars of your relationship to the teacher and the teaching. Nobody will force you to have that relationship. It is completely up to you. If you want to be connected to the teaching, you need to put effort into understanding the relationship and actualizing it. It is like wanting to be a citizen of a certain country. It is your choice whether you want to be a citizen or not. When you decide that you are going to be a citizen of a country, you are expected to abide by the principles and the regulations of that country.

One of the purposes of the Work is to encourage you to actualize and assert your true individuality. That does not mean to assert your individuality against the Work, because the Work is the very essence of that individuality. If you feel that you are asserting your individuality against the Work, what you are asserting is not your true individuality for the simple reason that the Work is what is helping you actualize true individuality. What you are asserting is your false personality; if you do not see that, the effort should go into seeing it, not into attempting to rationalize what you feel like doing. We need to see and acknowledge how the Work always functions as the lifeline for the real life. This means that your relationship to the teaching must be one of respect, consideration, love, appreciation, gratitude, and service at all times, regardless of your particular momentary feelings and opinions, because that is the attitude you need to have toward your essence. By understanding your relationship to the teaching, you will be able to actualize your true relationship to your essence, for the teaching is a true expression of Essence.

It is expected that various manifestations of the Work— tasks, aims, regulations, whatever—will produce certain reactions in you. Whatever the reactions are, they are to be understood and not acted out. Otherwise you are taking the side of your false personality against your essence. I do not mean that you should condemn or judge your reactions. No. You need to understand them. It is part of the Work to produce these reactions so you have a chance to look at them and study them. The Work is not doing something to you or for you. The Work is the way for you to be more yourself. The principles, ideas, concepts, and formulations of the Work come from the Essence that you are trying to actualize.

You need to see what you project onto the Work and what relationship that projection resembles. Any time you doubt the Work, object to some of its principles, or rebel against some of its regulations, and you identify with such attitudes, you are actually not benefiting from the Work. The channel is being closed by your actions. In the old times, it was said that you were not fit for the Work in such cases and didn't deserve it. I think that kind of judgment comes from the superego. It is better to say that your attitude is closing the door to your connection to Essence.

When you make the effort to understand your reactions to what happens here, you will always find an underlying unconscious issue, some kind of resistance. Sometimes it is hard to learn from these observations. Although you might have experienced them a thousand times, you identify with the emotions each time as if you didn't know better. Every time you identify with your reactions, it's as if you go to sleep.

You give time, energy, money for the Work. From the perspective of what you get, that's peanuts. Furthermore, it is very little time, energy, and money. Having a connection to your essence cannot be measured in these terms of time, energy, and money. Becoming real, finding out who you are and learning how to live as a real and genuine human being, cannot be measured by these things. When you are thinking about how much time or money you are giving, that thought itself is closing the channels because you are bartering with the Work.

In the old times, it was expected that the student give nothing less than everything—all his money, all his time, everything—because that was, and is, the most effective way. We don't ask that you do that here. We ask the minimum. But the principle stays the same. There are many stories where a master or teacher asks a student to give his life before he is given any teaching. It is that important. It is not possible to exaggerate how important the teacher is for the student.

You can't judge the importance of your essence because it is *you*. Without it, you are nothing. To understand that is the most important part of your work. We can see that it is not really possible for the student to judge the Work until he actually learns its principles in depth. You can have thoughts or ideas or opinions, but you cannot really judge it. So if you want to really benefit from the Work, you will need to understand all your judgments, all your opinions about it, so that you can be open to the nourishment that is needed for your kernel of Essence to grow. You need to question the Work sometimes, but that's to find the truth and to be able to be open to the truth.

It is necessary to consistently make the effort to set the Work over everything else. It is your path for realizing the preciousness in you. What is your life worth without your essence? What's the good of your business or your relationship or your sex life if you are not in touch with your essence, which is the source of all fulfillment? You can become a millionaire, have hundreds of lovers, whatever, but if you are not in touch with your essence, these things are useless, hollow. You can have all the ideas you want, but if they're not coming from your true nature, they're nothing. They are dust.

It's not a matter of trying to decide which is better right now: to do the Work or to do something else. The situation is never like that. When you truly understand what the Work is all about, you will see that the situation is always that the Work is the basis of real life. Whatever else you are going to do is useless if your essence is not in it. Don't kid yourself that you can do it by yourself, because most of the time your superego is in control and your unconscious is running your life. There is no way you can do this by yourself while your superego is in charge. You can tell yourself, "I don't really need the Work. I don't need anybody to help me. I'll find my own way." Some people get into that. But who's talking? You can do the Work on your own only if your essence is the center of your life already. If it is not, then you need a teaching or somebody who is connected to Essence.

If you really become clear about your relationship to the Work, that itself will do your work. The correct relationship to the teaching is to give to the teaching completely, without hesitation, to not expect anything back, and not even think you are giving. That is the correct relationship to the teaching. If you can achieve this, you are being your essence. I say that the correct relationship to the teaching is to give to the teaching. It is not because the teaching wants something from you. The teaching or the Work doesn't want or need anything from you.

It is a curious situation: There is this presence or source that doesn't want or need anything from you. At the same time, *you* need *it* for everything. Yet to get anything from it, you need to give it everything. That is exactly how Essence is. This is diametrically opposed to the way the unconscious and the ego function—not wanting to give anything, just wanting to be given to. Personality usually just wants to get. Even when it gives, it has to get something. It is usually calculating how much it's giving and how much it's getting. Essence doesn't do that. Essence gives and isn't thinking it is giving; it is not expecting anything back. Essence is the presence of satisfaction itself.

Having a correct relationship to the teaching will create the correct relationship to your essence. The beautiful thing is that if you accomplish this, you are being what you are looking for! So even in giving to the Work, you are being given to. That is the situation, and it must eventually be understood and actualized. To do this, you need to look at your unconscious and understand everything in it that creates an ambiguity about the Work. Regardless of how much you believe otherwise—and especially during those times when you believe otherwise—the most important thing is to make a great effort to disidentify from the feelings when you are feeling judgmental, opposed to the Work, or preferring something else. You need to disidentify and understand what is happening because it is during those very times that you are trying to defend against something very important in your unconscious, and your unconscious is fighting like hell for it. It's very rare when that is not the case when you are engaged in a real Work situation. When you approach a state of serious commitment to the Work—and therefore to yourself—it is very likely that your unconscious will raise hell because its job is to maintain the defenses that keep you away from your essence. So having these conflicts about the Work is a good opportunity to see what stands between you and your essence.

The Work, as I've said, doesn't want anything from you. However, the Work will take from you what needs to be taken. The Work will remove the weight from your shoulders, regardless of how much you are in love with your burden. Essence will take what weighs you down and give you yourself, nothing less. It is not as if the Work is doing you a favor by being nice to you or anything like that. The whole thing is very objective. It is lawful in that it follows a natural law.

The teacher is not sitting there feeling happy with himself because he took something from you or gave you something. It doesn't work like that. It's the same as when the rain falls and irrigates the land. The rain is not thinking, "Oh good! Look at all these trees growing up because of me." Rain just rains. That's its nature. It is true that rain is giving to the land, but the rain is not thinking of giving; it is not expecting to get rewards from it.

A large part of your Work is to understand and actualize your relationship to the teaching, to understand your barriers and conflicts about the regulations, rules, schedules, and all of that, and to attempt to have your relationship with the teacher and the Work as clear, as precise, as straight as possible. In practical terms, that means to see how you can accommodate or arrange your life so that you can harmonize with the schedules, how you can be punctual, how you can give your payment when you are asked for it. It means to always consciously, intentionally, remember to do these things, to remember the rules and regulations, and to do everything you can to actualize them. This is what is expected of you when you join any serious organization. It is even more important in the Work because of the nature of what you are to learn. By doing these things, you are learning to be a responsible human being. You are learning to have the correct relationship with your own essence. If you don't, you can't have a relationship with your own essence. You're always late for it. "Oh, let me do this other thing first; then I'll do it." That is already a preference of something else over your very nature. How is that going to work?

Of course, you need to be reasonable. Sometimes you have to be late for one reason or another that you have no control over. When you do have control over it, you have choices. That's when your work happens. That's when you can do some of the most important work on your personality through understanding your unconscious. Rules and schedules will change once in a while, precisely to bring out those reactions in you so that you can look at them. An example is the regulation I mentioned last time: that everybody who wants to be in the group will have to be at all meetings all the time, except for specific situations. That is done for you. What do I care? If you come less, I'll have less work. Why do I require you to come to every meeting? It is because we are looking at your situation and how you can do your work so that you benefit from the teaching in the most efficient and effective way. If I didn't care for you, I'd let you come once a month or once every two months. I wouldn't lose anything.

The correct relationship to the teaching is not a matter of blind obedience, although it was called "obedience to the teaching" in the old times. Ultimately, it is a *willing* obedience to the teaching and to your essence. It is obedience with an understanding of why a relationship of obedience is the one that works best. That understanding happens by understanding your unconscious. Learning to have the correct relationship to the teaching means learning how to be receptive, learning how to be a clear and unimpeded channel for the teaching. This clears the channel for your connection to your essence. The unconscious is what stands in the way.

By attempting to understand and actualize this relationship, you will confront all the parts of your unconscious— the feelings, opinions, prejudices, sensations, whatever patterns you have. These issues are to be looked at with disidentification. One way of looking at this process is that you need to understand your unconscious and your conflicts enough to be open so you can receive from the teaching. However, that is not the most accurate understanding of it. Working to understand the unconscious and the personal conflicts that are barriers against openness is, itself, the receiving. That is the giving, and that is the receiving. It is not that you work so that you will receive. The very work you do is the giving you do, and it is what you receive. The work itself *is* the process of transformation. The Work arranges situations in order to make that process happen. I don't mean that you are not receiving something besides the actual work you are doing. If you are connected to the Work, you are automatically receiving both in ways that you are aware of and ways you are not aware of. That is happening all the time. Your work makes the flow more steady. The nourishment is there; the substance of the teaching is present and available to you at all times. Your work can catalyze a certain alchemical reaction, the result of which will be the crystallization of certain substances that are your essence.

You've read in Ouspensky references to Gurdjieff talking about transformation of foods. That's what I'm talking about now. The food is there and can become food for your essence. A certain something has to happen; this is the work you do to understand yourself. Your work is the shock that is needed to put the substances into a new form, a finer form, which is your essence.

Usually, you do not see objectively. The accurate attunement to a teaching does not happen because you usually project your superego or your parents onto the teaching or onto the person of the teacher. That is the main impediment. You think the Work is your mother or father, and then you relate to the teaching or the teacher the way you related to them. You expect what you expected from your parents. You think that if I ask you to do a certain thing, my motivation is the same as what your father's or mother's would have been. So you have all these reactions and opinions, and you don't see clearly. If you try to understand this relationship, you'll be able to free yourself from having to relate according to the relationship with your parents.

It is not a matter of trying to trust the teaching or the teacher. If the teaching is real, then it is a matter of understanding what stops you from trusting. What you need to do is ask yourself, "What makes me feel this way? What are the influences in my unconscious that determine my attitude?" The reason you sometimes don't trust the teaching is often the same reason you don't trust your essence. Most of you still don't trust your essence. Most of you don't believe it will be enough to take care of you. You don't believe it is what you really need. You don't believe it is what really knows. You still prefer to listen to your mother.

So to have the correct attunement or the correct relationship to the teaching means you risk being unfaithful to your mother. It is your superego, it is your personality, it is your unconscious that you risk. Jesus said, "Leave your parents and follow me." That's what he meant, because you are usually listening to your mother. You try all the time to fight her—you argue, you get angry, all that—but you still listen. That is what you listen to all the time. Instead of listening to Jesus, people are listening to their mothers. Jesus had nothing against mothers and fathers. Jesus meant you should listen to the teachings present in your essence rather than listening to your superego.

What we come down to is dealing with faithfulness and loyalty to your parents. Most people are, at a deep level, very loyal and faithful. They will go through great suffering to avoid being disloyal to their parents, no matter how much they hate them. Sooner or later, the choice will be made: to be loyal to your conditioning and thus to the image of your parents in your unconscious or to be loyal to your essence, which gives you freedom and true security.

You have a chance here to have a truly genuine and direct relationship with a real human being—the teacher. It is probably the most real relationship you have in your life, and this can help you with your other relationships. It is an opportunity to live in a way that is truly and genuinely to your personal benefit instead of living according to the prejudices of your unconscious, which is not to your benefit.

If people don't go along with the regulations and the principles of the Work, I don't let them stay in the group. If they don't do the Work as instructed, obviously they will not learn, and there is no point in their staying. Why waste time?

I have noticed several patterns in students related to the Work rules. First, every time we change a regulation about something, some people object, some will not like it, and some will not comply. Then, I must do something to help people understand the rule. If I have to initiate the attempt to understand, that's fine with me. But then they have lost a chance to initiate the understanding themselves. Another thing I notice is that after a while, some people become lax;

they forget about the principles, the regulations, the schedule. Some people become loose about attendance and being punctual. Then I have to do something to cause them to start remembering. Again, if I do this, you lose the chance to learn something for yourself. I will continue reminding you of Work rules, but you need to learn to remind yourself. In time, you will need to be independent of the teacher. You will have the correct relationship on your own. You will want it; you will prefer it. You will be intentionally and consciously attuned to your essence and what is best for your essence.

S: I notice that how I do the Work depends on how I look at things. Most of the time, 99.99% of the time, I don't see anything except my superego, my trips, my desires. It is like a point in front of me that I fixate on, that pulls me. I want to understand this.

AH: What you usually feel is your personality. The best thing to do is to understand it, because understanding, or the attempt to understand, is the attunement to Essence, regardless of what it is you understand. The desire for understanding, the understanding itself, and the result of understanding are Essence. Do whatever is needed to understand your mind while remaining present. That, in itself, will attune you to your essence, to your true nature. It is not that you are looking for Essence; Essence is not something you are searching for. That is not how it works. You find Essence by *being* Essence through certain activities. This is so without your even knowing it. As your understanding increases and crystallizes, you start becoming aware of what it is that is increasing and crystallizing in you—your essence. It's not going to be something you get from somewhere over there. It's not as if Essence is a light somewhere and you walk in the dark until you find the light. The looking itself is going toward the light. By understanding, you embody the light more and more because understanding *is* the light.

S: Are you saying that in doing the Work, we should not look inside ourselves to find our essence?

AH: Right. You don't look for something. You look at what is there in your experience. If you are looking for *something*, that is an attitude of the unconscious. Most of the things that you want in your life can be found. In other words, the activity and the object are two different things, and generally, the activity leads to an object. Doing essential work is not like that. The activity is the object. When you are involved in your essence, it is not that understanding will lead you to something else. This lesson is hard to learn. The personality usually wants to function in terms of subject and object—an activity that will lead you some place. That's the habitual way the mind works. In terms of the Work, that is not really the correct attitude.

Here is a story about a Sufi teacher from *Tales of the Dervishes* by Idries Shah.

The Parable of the Greedy Sons

There was once a hard-working and generous farmer who had several idle and greedy sons. On his deathbed he told them that they would find his treasure if they were to dig in a certain field. As soon as the old man was dead, the sons hurried to the fields, which they dug up from one end to another, and with increasing desperation and concentration when they did not find the gold in the place indicated.

But they found no gold at all. Realizing that in his generosity their father must have given his gold away during his lifetime, they abandoned the search. Finally, it occurred to them that, since the land had been prepared, they might as well now sow a crop. They planted wheat, which produced an abundant yield. They sold this crop and prospered that year.

After the harvest was in, the sons thought again about the bare possibility that they might have missed the buried gold, so they again dug up the fields, with the same result.

After several years they became accustomed to labor, and to the cycle of the seasons, something which they had not understood before. Now they understood the reason for their father's method of training them, and they became honest and contented farmers. Ultimately they found themselves possessed of sufficient wealth no longer to wonder about the hidden hoard.

Thus it is with the teaching of the understanding of human destiny and the meaning of life. The teacher, faced with impatience, confusion and covetousness on the part of the students, must direct them to an activity which is known by him to be constructive and beneficial to them, but whose true function and aim is often hidden from them by their own rawness. (Idries Shah, *Tales of the Dervishes*, p. 144)

FIFTEEN

The Impeccable Warrior

We all have a purpose in being in the Work. Whatever our reasons are—a wish for freedom, realization, self-understanding—there are many ways to achieve our purpose. There are many paths, many schools, and many teachings. There are teachings of the mind, teachings of the heart, teachings of the belly. There are teachings of emptiness, teachings of awareness, teachings of absorption, teachings of love, teachings of compassion, teachings of will. In many, the path focuses on one of these aspects along with certain methods, formulations, techniques, and concepts particular to that one aspect. Each aspect that I mentioned—emptiness, awareness, love, compassion, and so on—is one part of the whole picture. Each aspect, in a sense, forms one facet of the same diamond. So all facets are part of the same thing. All the teachings, the different paths, lead to the same place.

The teaching of a certain facet—the teaching of Truth, for example—is a specialization based on that particular aspect. It uses a particular approach to arrive at Truth and the same approach to arrive at all the other aspects. Occasionally a teaching can be based on more than one aspect or facet. It can include several together. If you follow any one of those teachings, you have to follow it with total dedication and ignore the other paths. The other paths will be a distraction.

Which do we have in our Work here? We call our method "The Diamond Approach." We don't call it "The Truth Approach," "The Love Approach," or "The Will Approach." We call it "The Diamond Approach" for a particular reason. This teaching is like a many-faceted diamond. Our approach is not a specialization of one or even several facets. It is not a specialization of truth or compassion or emptiness, although we are concerned with all these aspects. We use the teaching of truth, the teaching of love, the teaching of clarity, of will, of compassion and the like, without focusing on any one of them exclusively. What we do is to use all the facets to create a balanced whole. We look from many different perspectives; we experience the same thing from all possible angles.

If we have a specialization, it is the diamond as a whole, not one of its facets. We don't take one attitude and focus on it by itself. We learn instead to work with various aspects and to balance them. We see, for instance, that surrender is important and useful, but we also see that curiosity about the truth is important and useful. We see that determination and will are useful. We also see that clarity is useful. All need to be taken together to form a balanced attitude which, ultimately, is not an attitude, but the absence of an attitude.

We explore the various facets, the various attitudes, to create the right attitude needed for people in the group. Sometimes we talk about compassion; sometimes we talk about truth; sometimes we talk about will; sometimes we talk about peace. It depends on the over-all need. I want to remind you that these discussions have a very definite and practical purpose. They are not just for theoretical stimulation. Today I will talk about a certain aspect, a certain facet, that I haven't talked about before. It is an attitude, an understanding, and a perception that is necessary to do the work we're doing. Without it, this work is difficult and not as effective.

In the Diamond Approach, each facet, each essential aspect, has a corresponding deficiency or "hole." Today we'll talk about one of these holes which is usually present all the time, to see how we can best deal with it. This hole is revealed when you confront your indulgence. Indulgence is what permits the weak part of you to run the strong part of you. Indulgence is allowing what is unhealthy in you to control your life even when you *know* it is unhealthy. Indulgence is being lazy about what you know you need to do, allowing the usual automatic tendencies to dominate and run your life. Indulgence is the enemy of certainty.

So, let's start from the beginning. Obviously, you have come here to do certain work. You know that something is missing in your life, or that your life is not going the way you want it to go or think it should go. For reasons which are conscious or unconscious, you come here because you know there is something that needs to be done, something that needs to be understood, something that needs to be changed. This is an accurate perception. Almost everybody needs to do some work because everybody's life is, in a sense, a mess. The more you work on yourself, the more you see how much of a mess it is. Usually, in the beginning you won't let yourself see how much of a mess you are in because the impact would be too great. So you take little peeks. You see a little mess here, a little mess there. You discover that almost all the corners are quite a mess. Of course, the more you see that your life is a mess, the more there is an impetus, an impulse, to do something about bringing in order, cleanliness, room for clean air.

You're presented with certain methods, certain concepts, certain teachings, and you do certain practices to understand yourself, to tidy up the mess. As you go further, you understand what you need to do. Many times you know just what the difficulty is and what needs to be done. A lot of times you know of a certain weakness, a certain inadequacy you have in terms of dealing with your life. You know something needs to be done there. You learn about your unconscious and how it's been running your life. In a sense, you get pretty much all the tools you need to work on yourself in the first few months of coming to these group meetings.

But what do you usually do? You have the tools, you have the information, you have the understanding. Do you then set about doing it with complete commitment and diligence? If you're like most students, you give maybe an hour a day. The rest of the time, what do you do? Indulge in the habits and tendencies that you know are detrimental to your freedom, to your development, to your expansion, even to your health. You know the problem, but you continue the old ways. If you look at yourself, you will see that tendency. After a certain time of self-study, you will know your main patterns that keep you from the freedom you seek, but most of the time you continue to follow them anyway.

For instance, you might have a pattern of always falling in love with a person you know is going to reject you. You've done this twenty times; you know it very well. Then two people present themselves. You know one of them will reject you, and one of them will not reject you. You automatically choose the one who will reject you, no?

Here is another example. Let's say you always have a tendency to be busy, and you know being busy helps you avoid certain things. You've seen it thirty times. You've had sixty-five insights about it. Five minutes after your sixty-fifth insight, you're doing the same thing. Busy, wasting time, fooling around. What happened to the sixty-five insights? You're waiting for the sixty-sixth.

Or take meditation. You know that meditation is one of the things we do fifteen to twenty minutes a day, and you know it's useful. You know that every time you do it, you benefit from it. But instead of getting up and doing your meditation, you stay in bed. Or a friend calls, and you go out for breakfast. Or you're actually meditating and the phone rings, so you interrupt your meditation to answer it. This is going along with your habitual patterns; it's indulgence. You might even be indulging in something you know is actually harmful. You know you might die the next day from doing it, and you still continue doing it. Or maybe you take an aim, and you do it sometimes but not other times. When you do it, you do it half way. You know you could do it well, but you don't do your best.

Indulgence can be indulgence in anything. You could be indulging in your laziness, indulging in your depression, your fear, your paranoia, indulging in being busy, indulging in attacking yourself or other people, indulging in self-criticism and criticizing other people, indulging in avoiding things, indulging in postponing things, indulging in gossip. Any attitude, feeling, or unconscious tendency of your personality can be used as an indulgence. That is one of the qualities of the personality: to keep on indulging. Even when you know it really is just your personality, even when you know it's something you picked up along the way and serves no good purpose, you continue doing it. You know, for instance, that your fear has no foundation in reality, but the next time a situation presents itself, you act according to that fear. You act in the same way, following the same pattern.

You have come here to work on yourself. At least you tell yourself you're here to work on yourself, to free yourself. But how can you free yourself when you keep indulging yourself? Freeing yourself is not easy. It may be the most desirable undertaking in the world, but it's also the most difficult. It requires a lot of sustained, continual work. When I say work, I don't mean sustained, continual seriousness. I mean really doing what you need to do to free yourself, to understand yourself and your patterns—including your patterns of indulgence. Some of you may use what I'm saying now as ammunition for the superego to bombard you more. "Hah, indulgence! Bad, bad, bad!" You keep indulging in attacking yourself. I'm not telling you this so you can use it to beat yourself up.

So indulgence is going along with a tendency or an attitude that you know is detrimental to your freedom, your health, or your development. The result is that you don't take responsibility for yourself. You don't take your life in your own hands. Implied in this is that you are waiting for a savior. A savior could be any number of things: an insight, a blessing, a person, or the attitude that things will change in time. Time becomes a savior. But that belief is an indulgence, and you will know it's an indulgence just by looking around at some of the people who are in their seventies and eighties. Has time changed them? Usually it does change them—in the wrong direction. The patterns don't dissolve; they calcify.

So what can we do? What is the best way to go about dealing with indulgence? Essentially, what indulgence amounts to is that you're not taking responsibility for the regulation of your own system. You expect somebody else, or time, or God, or whatever, to do it for you. It is the same attitude as the infant who does not know how to regulate itself and

depends on something external—the mother in this case—
to clean it and feed it, to release its tension, comfort it, and
all that. For a baby, it is not an indulgence because a baby
cannot do it for himself. The mother has to do it. But being
an adult means taking care of yourself, doing what you
know is best for your system. Indulgence covers up this deficiency of self-regulation, including autonomic regulation.

S: Where I'm trapped is that I often identify all pleasure with indulgence. I'm wondering if you could make a
distinction between pleasure that is an indulgence and
pleasure that is healthy.

AH: Indulgence usually has to do with being taken care
of and the expectation of pleasure. The origin of indulgence
is that state when mother did things for you and made you
feel better. So when you are indulging yourself, it's a way
of trying to be close to mother. Something about her is near
you; some kind of sweetness is in the air. You're opting for
that little murky sweetness, that little obscure pleasure of
somebody regulating you, like wiping your ass. When you
were a little baby and took a shit, your mother came and
wiped your ass. She took care of you, and it felt wonderful. So when you're an adult and you make a mess, any
kind of mess, or you have some kind of a problem, and
you expect somebody else to take care of it, to clean it up,
to wipe your ass—that's indulgence. Indulgence is usually
fueled by a kind of obscure pleasure. It's not real pleasure,
but a feeling that makes you feel close to mother. It reminds
you of the time when you were taken care of. It's an expectation of being taken care of.

We see now how indulgence can be an obstacle, a barrier to your work and to your freedom. The work of freeing yourself needs a lot of dedication, a lot of determination.
It needs your best effort. If you're not doing your best,
you're indulging. If you're indulging, your personality has
the upper hand.

So what do we do about our indulgences, about our tendencies and attitudes and actions that we know are not good for us and that keep us trapped in our personality? Learning how to deal with indulgence means you must have a certain perspective, a certain attitude toward your life and work. It has to do with how you take action, what you do at any given moment.

This brings us to a method that deals primarily with indulgence: the path of the warrior. When you are working on yourself, you need the attitude of the warrior. Not the worrier, the warrior. You need to live the life of the impeccable warrior. To really do the Work, to really be able to succeed, you need to live and work like an impeccable warrior. Everything needs to be done with impeccability. Every attitude, every task, every aim needs to be done impeccably.

Now what does that mean? To do something impeccably doesn't mean to do it perfectly. Let's look at some examples of what it does mean. Suppose you know you need to work on a certain tendency; for example, you want to stop trying to please other people all the time. Perhaps you take an aim not to try to please other people. How can you do that impeccably? It means you do the best you can in terms of that aim, always, at all times.

This requires many things. First of all, it requires awareness. You need to pay attention to yourself so you can catch the impulses, the desires, the feelings of wanting to please somebody else. It doesn't mean you have to be aware of everything, of every single thing all the time, because that is not possible. You cannot be aware of everything at every single moment. Being impeccable means doing all that you can do at that moment. It means doing your best, your very best. Let's say you're paying attention, and somebody you like passes by. Here's the test. Are you going to be impeccable or are you going to be an indulging infant? If you're indulgent, you take a vacation from your aim. You say, "I feel good about this guy. This guy is different. The aim doesn't matter in this case; there's no need to pay that much attention." Before you know it, you're kissing his ass.

To be impeccable at that moment is to do all that you can do to pay attention, to use whatever you have learned, especially at those times when you know you have a tendency to not pay attention. Your knowledge is not perfect, not complete, but you use what you know, the best techniques you have, the best attitude you have, the best understanding you have, and apply it right then. You know, for instance, that the best thing you can do is to sense, look, and listen. So, you sense, look, and listen to the best of your ability at that time—not to ninety percent of your ability, but to one hundred percent of your ability. You use all your ability, all your wisdom, all the knowledge you have. This is the way of the impeccable warrior.

Let's take the schedule here as an example. You know the meetings start at 7:30. You are having dinner. You are about fifteen minutes from here. The meeting is at 7:30 and it is now 7:10. You're finishing and you say, "I think I'll have some dessert." You can tell by looking at the situation objectively that it will take you ten minutes to have dessert, which means you'll be five minutes late. So what do you do? Impeccability has the sharpness of a razor's edge. You are impeccable, or you are not. Five minutes can make the difference. You are impeccable or indulging. Sometimes you might try to avoid choosing by using some kind of lack of clarity: "Oh well, I don't know. It might just take five minutes to finish my dessert." If you really looked clearly, you'd know. But you don't want to know. You want to indulge.

Now, an impeccable warrior doesn't have to go without dessert. An impeccable warrior might order a dessert and take it with him and eat it in the car. The point is not about having or not having dessert. The point is to be on time. It is not about self-denial or any kind of punishment. You want to do things in a way that will work for you so that the part of you that is healthy will be in charge, not the part of you that is indulging. Not the infantile part that keeps you the way you are. To act in an impeccable way requires many things, including understanding, knowledge, and will.

Let's say you are working on disidentification. You have just learned how much you identify with your emotions. How are you going to be impeccable as you learn how to disidentify? To be impeccable as you work on disidentifying with your emotions means to work on disidentification all the time. It means always paying attention and being aware of what's happening. It doesn't mean paying attention once and then saying, "That's enough for today" or "This is too difficult right now; I think I'll go to a movie. Maybe I don't really need to disidentify so much after all. Maybe I'll do some disidentifying later." No. If you want to work on disidentification, you do it. That's it—no vacations. No dropping it and leaving it behind.

However, being impeccable can mean taking certain kinds of vacations. We all need vacations from what we're doing, even though we may be doing what is healthiest for us. Let's say you're learning to disidentify from your emotions and you're getting to a place in your work that is difficult. You don't know if you can handle it any more; you don't know if you can still give it your full attention. How can you take a vacation and still be impeccable? It is a very simple matter. You don't just stop paying attention. You make a clear-cut decision for yourself: " For the next two hours, it is all right if I don't work on disidentifying." You take your vacation, your indulgence, impeccably. Who decides? You, not your indulgence. You are acknowledging your limitations, not excusing yourself. You're giving your indulgence space, but the indulgence is not running you. You have made a conscious choice. You stay impeccable.

When you're learning to defend against your superego, you really need to be an impeccable warrior. You can't do it in a haphazard way. You can't do it one time and not another, a little bit now, a little bit later. It won't work. You have to do it constantly, all the time. Impeccably. That means if you really want to learn about defending against your superego, you make it your number one aim. "For the next three weeks, I'm going to learn how to defend against my superego." This means that during those three weeks you're going to do it impeccably. You are always aware of defending against your superego, and you do your best. You do not do your best for half an hour and then spend the rest of the day involved in the usual attacks. If you want your aim to work, that's what needs to happen. If you don't give your aim your full and constant attention, if you indulge yourself, the one who indulges will be strengthened. It is the infant in you, the part of you that does not want to be responsible. That part will continue to run your life. This is not a moral judgment; nobody is going to punish you. It's just how things happen. The attitude of the impeccable warrior is a certain facet, a certain perspective that needs to be present for the Work to be effective.

S: I get confused about knowing when my superego is beating me up and when I know I need to be impeccable. It's hard to tell the difference.

AH: I was sure that question would come up. That question is probably arising in the minds of most of you because it is very hard to understand what being impeccable is. On the subtle level of learning to be impeccable, what will arise is the issue of uncertainty. You're not certain; you're not sure. "Is this the right way, or is that the right way?" "What does it mean to be impeccable now?" "Is this really impeccability, or is it my superego?" "Am I really indulging, or am I being impeccable?" Things get a little tricky. The personality has its powers and its subtleties. But you see, this is exactly what I was saying. You cannot be perfect in it. Doing things perfectly is not the point. The point is doing your best. If you are not certain, you have two ways to go: this way or that way. The impeccable thing is to take the attitude of the impeccable warrior when the warrior is uncertain. To deal with uncertainty *impeccably*, you do the best you can do in the situation. At the moment of uncertainty, you might need to pay more attention to yourself, to take the attitude of the detached observer instead of deciding to go this way or that way.

Uncertainties will arise, especially when it comes to learning how to *be*, how to act as an impeccable warrior. As I said earlier, uncertainty is the enemy of impeccability. It is the most subtle enemy. Uncertainty is due to incomplete awareness, incomplete knowledge of what is there. This will often arise because you rarely know everything about a situation. That is exactly when the attitude of impeccability is needed. It is not to be perfect, but to do your best to act according to all the wisdom, all the understanding, all the experience, all the awareness, all the will that you have.

As you confront your indulgences, you will see that to continue to be really impeccable and not succumb to your indulgences will mean letting go of all kinds of things. The way of impeccability can be taken as a path on its own. You could attempt to be impeccable all the time. All your indulgences would arise, and these would reveal all your attachments. Impeccability means letting go of those attachments.

The way of the impeccable warrior is complete in itself. It is a path to a certain knowledge. In our Work here, we're not taking that path by itself, but we're using it. We're taking that attitude as an aid. That aspect, that perspective, that facet, has a certain point of view, a certain way of looking at things that is needed for our Work to be effective.

As we have described, being impeccable is to be and do your best at every moment. At those times when you feel you cannot do your best, you can still do your best by impeccably deciding you will take some time off. This applies to everything you do. To live impeccably means to live impeccably in all tasks, in all aims, in all undertakings, whether you're learning to defend against your superego or learning to be present all the time. Each one of these needs to be done impeccably for it to actually work. It is the perspective of a certain aspect of Essence that is needed for all the other aspects. As we have seen, indulgence will arise along with uncertainty, and your indulgence and uncertainty will try to stop you from being an impeccable warrior.

To be impeccable is to be realistic. You don't expect from yourself what you cannot do; you expect the best you can do. Because the way of impeccability will bring up all kinds of uncertainties and unsureness, you will ultimately learn certainty because you will have to deal with those uncertainties. In time, impeccability will become certainty. You become certain in yourself. You have a certainty that has nothing to do with your mind.

So, to act impeccably means to act with certainty. You cannot act impeccably when you are not sure of yourself. You know what the best thing is, and you do it with certainty, even if you know that it is not perfect. You're learning to defend against your superego. Maybe you are not completely sure what this means, but you know something. And since what you know is the best you know, you do this as if you are certain. You do this until you learn something else. In time, this attitude will evolve into what we call true certainty, essential certainty.

Choosing to be an impeccable warrior means choosing to be a responsible adult instead of being your mother's baby. There is dignity in it; you are your own person. Your life is your responsibility, and you always have the choice to do your best.

Impeccability can be in action, in feeling, in thinking. Impeccability can be in terms of the will, in terms of the mind, in terms of the heart. One of the times when some people will become most uncertain about impeccability is when it comes to the heart—where there is softness and gentleness and delicacy—because impeccability seems to imply something sharp and straight. But you can be impeccable about love. This means that you have some understanding about your attractions and their patterns, what's positive in them and what's negative. And in this case, to be impeccable means to act according to the knowledge you have about these things. You might know, for instance, that you always give up your heart for the sake of approval, or pleasure, or security, and you know this always creates a mess. In this case, to act impeccably means to go against the usual inclinations of your heart because your heart is not free, not impeccable on its own.

A warrior is always alert, always doing her best to be alert. You can't be a warrior and indulge in being spaced out. A warrior is engaged in matters of life and death. This is a correct perspective in regard to work on yourself. It is not the only way of looking at it, but it is one of the attitudes that is needed as a thread throughout your work.

Of course, not everybody will want to be an impeccable warrior. Not everybody believes it is necessary. If being free from your personality is not the most important thing to you, you will not choose to be impeccable. You can simply continue indulging yourself, and nobody is going to punish you.

You either need to work on getting your life together or your life is already together. Maybe at some point you don't need to work on it. But it's not as if you work on yourself, learn to be impeccable, and after you learn to be impeccable, then it's okay to indulge. If you've really done it, if you've learned to be an impeccable warrior and you've arrived at certainty, then maybe you don't need to put effort into getting your life together because you're doing it naturally and harmoniously and spontaneously without any effort. That doesn't mean you're indulging. You see, if you are an impeccable warrior and you have arrived at essential certainty, indulgences don't come back. If the wish to indulge returns, then you need to continue working because you still have issues about responsibility and certainty.

If you are an impeccable warrior, you do not look to the future. Every minute you have a task. You're completely dedicated to that task and you are not thinking of the result. You don't have time; you are too busy being impeccable. The result will happen without your thinking about it. If you're thinking about the result, you're not impeccable.

To be an impeccable warrior, you do your tasks impeccably. Your task is to be impeccable. That's it. You do your best. After a while, you are impeccable for the sake of impeccability itself. I've talked about it in terms of a path leading someplace, but it is actually what we are going toward. It's both the means and the end. When you are really impeccable, that's it. It's not as if you're looking for truth because truth will lead you to something else. No. You're dedicated to the truth because the truth is truth. It is the same thing with impeccability.

S: I think I'm making this idea of the impeccable warrior into an image and saying, "I will be free when I am an impeccable warrior." I'm beginning to sense that that in itself is a form of indulgence, kind of like putting it off.

AH: Being impeccable means you're not thinking of being something in the future. It means you're doing something right now. You're sitting. How do you sit impeccably? How do you listen impeccably? How do you ask questions impeccably? Impeccability is concerned with now, with complete presence at every moment. You are either impeccable or you are not. Part of impeccability is taking limitations into consideration because if you don't, you're indulging. You take your limitations into consideration as much as you can. Impeccability is not judged by superego. It is judged by reality, what's really there. If there is something that can be done, you do it. You do your best at every moment.

SIXTEEN

Curiosity

The People Who Attain

Imam el-Ghazali relates a tradition from the life of Isa, ibn Maryam.

Isa one day saw some people sitting miserably on a wall, by the roadside.

He asked, "What is your affliction?"

They said, "We have become like this through our fear of hell."

He went on his way, and saw a number of people grouped disconsolately in various postures by the wayside. He said, "What is your affliction?" They said, "Desire for Paradise has made us like this."

He went on his way, until he came to a third group of people. They looked like people who had endured much, but their faces shone with joy.

Isa asked them, "What has made you like this?"

They answered: "The Spirit of Truth. We have seen Reality, and this has made us oblivious of lesser goals."

Isa said, "These are the people who attain. On the Day of Accounting these are they who will be in the Presence of God." (Idries Shah, *Tales of the Dervishes*, p. 181)

This story describes our Work in a nutshell. It illustrates the method and the meaning of the Work. It tells the main difficulties people get into that stop them from doing the Work, and it relates the path to the goal, the Work to attainment.

The method of the Work, the path, the stages, and the final result are all one thing. This story tells us what that is. Usually you imagine that you will work until you get someplace; then you'll be happy. This is a misunderstanding. It is a misunderstanding of what happiness is and of what brings about happiness. This misunderstanding leads to a wrong orientation. As long as you have this misunderstanding, you'll be barking up the wrong tree. The truth in this story must be learned over and over again until it becomes your guiding principle. Most people don't like to hear it; they would like things to be otherwise. However, if you really think about it, you'll see why it couldn't be otherwise. It is the truth in the story that is really the main principle and method of this Work. It is also what makes life interesting and rich. What is there throughout all the stages is also the end. So the end is there all the time.

Now we'll go back to the story and see what the story is talking about. Isa, ibn Maryam means "Jesus, son of Mary." This story is about Jesus encountering three groups of people. Only one group are the people who attain.

The first group of people seem to be having a hard time, suffering and not knowing how to get out of that suffering. They are having a hard time because of their fear of hell. Their fear of hell has led them to a state of continuous misery. Hell, as everyone knows, is the state of pain and suffering. People who are afraid of hell, or want to get away from hell, are people who don't want to suffer. Conversely, people who don't want to experience pain or suffering, people who don't want to experience anguish or conflict, people who don't want to experience anxiety or hurt are the people who are afraid of hell. Hell is just a symbol or representation of what we see as difficult or painful. Hell is saying, "No, I don't want this. I want to get out of here! Get me out of here! It's too much— I can't stand it! It's too painful."

The story tells us something very important about that strategy. It tells us that this strategy keeps us in hell even more. Resistance to hell is actually the best way to stay in hell. Not wanting to suffer is the shortest road to suffering.

Now, of course, most of you don't want to hear that. That is why you might understand it for a day but then say, "Let me out of here! If there is pain, I don't want to see it! I don't want to experience it!" It is the movement of pushing things away, of resisting them and trying to get away from them, that generates pain.

The second group seem to be the opposite. They are interested in paradise; they want to go to heaven. They are always looking for happiness, doing all kinds of things so that finally the day will come when the doors of heaven will open and they will enter with glory and live happily ever after. The story tells us that those people are just as unsuccessful as the first kind of people. Both trying to avoid hell and trying to get to heaven seem to produce suffering, to perpetuate anguish. If you look at your life, you will see these movements of your mind in every minute—you are trying to get away from pain and go toward pleasure.

This is not a lesson on morals; we are just seeing how things work. You might not like the laws of nature or the laws of the universe, but they are the laws, and you are the product of those laws. You can try to get away from suffering or go toward pleasure, but as the story says—and I think there is a lot of evidence to substantiate it—that attitude seems to perpetuate your pain and suffering. Your fear of hell and desire for paradise both bring suffering.

We can relate this discussion to attachment. If you don't want to experience your pain, there is an attachment. If you want to experience pleasure, there is an attachment. Do you remember what we said attachment was? It is the pure substance of hell itself. It is pure, unadulterated anguish. Anguish is exactly what is produced by the movement of attachment. The movement of attachment always occurs in one of two ways: either a movement away from pain or a movement toward pleasure. Regardless of how you might try to get out of this dilemma, you won't. If you have either of these two attitudes—which are actually one attitude—you are caught in the dilemma. You can't get out of a sticky situation by becoming stickier. No matter how many times I say this or how many times I read the stories, you will not get it unless you make this understanding your practice every minute of your life, as much as possible. It is the truth and we know it is the truth, but it is not an easy matter to do anything but remain stuck in these attitudes, as you all know.

If you look at your experience at this very moment, you'll find that most likely you're either in some kind of painful state that you don't want to experience or in something good you do want to experience and hold on to. That very attitude is bound to bring pain and suffering. The very core of the personality, what makes the personality a personality, is that state of attachment that brings with it the state of anguish. This state of attachment and anguish is a result of the attitude of avoiding pain and going after pleasure and, also, is the very movement away from pain and toward pleasure. Indulging in that attitude perpetuates and strengthens the personality. It can't help but do that. That attitude is food for suffering—and for your personality.

The personality doesn't know what else to do if it doesn't do these two things. "If I don't try to get something good or get away from something bad, what else is there?" It's true that the personality doesn't know what else to do because the personality is based on this very attitude. The personality develops because of this attitude. Freud called it "the pleasure principle." The personality is built on the pleasure principle, on avoidance of pain and going towards pleasure.

These attitudes go all the way through your personality, through all the levels of your consciousness. It can be a very subtle thing. It is not a matter of saying, "Okay, now I'm not going to avoid pain, and I'm not going to go towards pleasure." If you look carefully at what you would want from this policy, you'll find that you want some kind of pleasure, probably some kind of release. Some people want to use this strategy to avoid pain. So there is a movement, a desire, which is based on the lack of complete welcoming and accepting of what is there, of what our consciousness is presented with. We are given the opportunity to experience all kinds of things. Our mind says, "This is bad, and this is good. All I want is the good; I don't want the bad." Yet we are presented with the whole thing.

This situation, the dilemma of always acting from the perspective of good and bad and not knowing how to act differently, is one that everyone is in. You don't have to be working on yourself to be in that dilemma. This truth is operating whether you are eighty years old or ten years old, whether you are married or single, whether you are taking a shit or eating food or making love or fighting with someone, whether you are driving your car or riding in an airplane, whether you are walking or sitting, thinking or falling alseep. Whatever you are doing, this principle is operating and causing you to suffer. Whether you are working for success, achievements, and riches, working on understanding yourself, or having a hard time in your life, this principle is the truth that is operating. It is omnipresent. It controls your personality, your consciousness, and your life.

You don't have to be wanting to work on yourself to see that this is your situation. Everybody is in the same boat. You're always trying to be happy, and you end up being miserable. You're always trying to get away from pain, and you get more pain. The mind can't make sense of this. How can you be happy if you don't try to be happy? But that is the problem—that you want to be happy. If you want to be happy, you are already operating from the perspective of pain.

It is a truth most people don't like. It seems it would be much better if it were otherwise. It would be much easier if you could get happiness by going toward happiness, and if pain would go away when you tried to go away from it. It seems as if this would be wonderful. But you need to look at the reality, whether you like it or not. What can you do, rebel? If you rebel, you'll just suffer more.

You could decide to change it, but it's not going to change. You can deny it for years and years and suffer until your pain catches up with you. Then you might say, "Well, there must be something that's not right here. What I have been doing with my life isn't working. Let me try to find the meaning of life, the secret of existence, the secret of happiness." It's very tricky. You may decide to do some spiritual work, but why do you want to do that? If you do it with that attitude, you'll suffer even more. You say, "No, I want to do spiritual work. I want to do the Diamond Approach and meditate because I want to realize my essence. I want to be enlightened." Why? Why do you want to be enlightened? What do you have in mind?

You want to feel good, right? You heard someone talk about Essence, and now you believe Essence will give it to you, Essence will open the door of heaven for you. "Now I'm going to get my essence, and it will be the best thing that ever happened—the best, most perfect mommy that I've ever had. It will take care of me; my life will feel wonderful."

It is true that Essence could do that, but not from the perspective you're looking from. Because that attitude is, by itself, a misunderstanding of Essence. When you experience Essence, you'll see that Essence doesn't feel that it wants this or that. It isn't busy pushing away pain or going toward happiness. Essence is just there, experiencing—no rejection and no acceptance. Just presence.

So far we've talked about the first two groups in the story, which covers the situation of almost everybody. Now let's try to understand the third group, the group who are released from the conflict, finally are able to transcend the movement of desire and attachment—the people who know the secret. The most important thing to understand here is what the secret of this group is. How did they end up shining with joy while the other people suffered? I'll reread that part.

> Isa asked them, "What has made you like this?"
> They answered: "The Spirit of Truth. We have seen Reality, and this has made us oblivious of lesser goals."

They say nothing of wanting pain or not wanting pain, of wanting pleasure or not wanting pleasure. It's not relevant for them. What's the point of being concerned with what feels good and what feels bad? Curious, isn't it? What do they do? How do they do it? The story tells us how they describe their state, but it is not easy to understand what the words really mean.

Some people might say that these people want truth. The story does not say that they want truth. It doesn't say that they want anything. There's no mention of any movement toward anything. There isn't even a movement toward truth. Some people say, "We're doing the Work because we want the truth, and the truth will set us free." Other stories say that, but this story does not say that. It does not say the truth will set you free. It does not say that people want truth, or look for truth, or seek truth. It says nothing about that.

It does mention truth in a particular way. The truth is in the resolution, in the correct understanding. We're all learning to see the truth; that's what everybody here does. But why do you want to see the truth? Did you ever ask yourself that? What do you want from it? If you ask yourself that at any moment, you'll find out that you're seeking truth either to avoid pain or to have pleasure. "I will experience my wonderful essence, and I will be released. Ah!" That's not really different from having sex with your lover. The means are different, but it's the same process. This story says that process will ultimately lead you to more stickiness, more suffering.

The third group not only gives us something that will lead us someplace, but it tells us the meaning and point of our Work. It shows us the attitude and the experience that happen when people actually live in a way that is not concerned about these two things. We don't do this Work so that you'll get something that will release you and then you'll feel happy. It doesn't work that way. As we've seen, doing it that way is exactly what leads to suffering.

Before we examine the truth of this third group, you need to first realize how attached you are to the first two attitudes, how much they really dominate your life and your mind and your personality, how you really do not know yourself apart from these attitudes. You don't really recognize how much you live this way, afraid of pain and wanting pleasure; how full of anger and rage you are that reality does not run the way you want it; how hurt you are that the world does not go according to the way you *will* it to be; how frustrated you are about this, how you continue not wanting to listen to the truth. The attachments are very powerful; they run your life. That needs to be understood as deeply and completely as possible until you understand and accept the truth of the third group. It is a subtle truth but a very simple one. It could be understood at any moment. It is within everyone's grasp.

This story is more exact than the stories that describe the path as "seeking after truth." It's about "the spirit of truth." What is "the spirit of truth?" How does the spirit of truth by itself lead to joy? The spirit of truth is the attitude that transcends the experience of the first two groups.

The third group accepts the truth. The truth could be painful or pleasurable. The affect of it, the emotional shading of it, is irrelevant. Truth is what is there. Pleasure and pain are irrelevant to it. These are judgments of our personality. What actually exists is the truth. What is presented to your consciousness all the time is the truth. This will help us understand why the first two attitudes lead to pain and suffering. To try to avoid pain and to always seek pleasure will mean the nonacceptance of truth much of the time. It involves the rejection of what is there. You are rejecting your experience. You are rejecting your consciousness. You are rejecting yourself. How is that going to lead to harmony and happiness? Sometimes your experience is painful. What are you going to do? It's your experience. If you don't want it, you have to throw it away. Then you throw away part of yourself. Well, how can you be happy if part of yourself has been thrown away? Bringing in this perspective of truth helps us to understand why the first two attitudes don't work.

What if a person says, "I will seek the truth, and the truth will set me free. Since seeking truth is not the same as avoiding pain or seeking pleasure, then I'm not acting according to that principle." Sounds good, but why do you want the truth? How come you're suddenly interested in truth when you haven't been all these years? We talk about truth, and suddenly you're for truth. Why? What do you want from it? People who do the Work for a long time have the attitude: "I want to seek the truth. I'll go through pain, I'll continue whether there's pleasure or not." But often the more you seek the truth, the more pain there is. Obviously, you're doing something wrong, because you're not getting the joy that the third group got.

If you look at it, most of the time when you are seeking truth, you are really one of those people who wants to avoid pain and find pleasure. Now you're riding in a different kind of car, the golden car, and you think that's going to get you there. You wonder, "How come I'm still suffering?" But you haven't done anything. You've changed from one car to another. You might be learning all kinds of truth— about your parents, your self, your emotions, your personality, your essence—all of that. You feel good now and then, although sometimes you feel miserable, and things are dramatic and exciting and intense. You experience holes of deficiency, fountains of essential experience, all of that. But the picture doesn't seem to change much; it just gets more intense. The pain is more painful, and the pleasure is more pleasurable. You might get more subtle then and say, "Aha! That's what I've been doing! I've been seeking truth for pleasure's sake—for the pleasure of my personality. That's why the picture continues to be the same. It's true I've been seeking truth, but I'm really doing it to get pleasure, and that's not the real teaching of truth."

Perhaps you go to a mountain top and talk to a guru. You tell him you've finally found the reason why you're suffering—that it's not a matter of just seeking truth, but that seeking truth for pleasure is the same old thing. The guru very wisely says, "You have seen the truth." When you ask, "What is the teaching of truth?" the guru answers that it is to seek truth for its own sake. "Ah, I've got it! Thank you, guru! From now on I'll seek truth for its own sake." So you open all your books, start reading and meditating. "I don't care about pain or pleasure. I just want the truth! I am going to seek truth. From now on, I am a truth seeker, a truth fan."

The guru told you the right thing—to seek truth for its own sake. But why do you want to seek truth for its own sake? There's nothing in your personality that wants to do this. Later, you go back to the guru and ask, "How come it doesn't work? I've been seeking truth for its own sake and the more I do it, the heavier my mind gets. I can hardly hold my head up, it's so full of truth. I am getting sadder and more miserable." He says, "Gee, I don't know what went wrong. You were seeking truth for its own sake."

This particular transition is very delicate and important. The teaching of the guru was somewhat true, but it was not exact. In the story, the answer is the spirit of truth. They don't say that the spirit of truth is to seek truth. We can understand more by asking ourselves why we believed the guru when he told us to seek truth for its own sake. What motivated us? Why did we suddenly become truth seekers? Someone tells you to seek truth, so right away you seek truth? Why? Why did you ask the guru what would lead to realization? What was your motivation? You will see that your motivation was still the motivation of the first group.

I will go over several considerations that lead us to the understanding of the spirit of truth. First of all, truth is really more the realm of the heart than the realm of the mind. Truth is not a mental thing. When you discover the Truth aspect of Essence, you find it is a heart quality. What makes you know that something is true is a sense in the heart, not in the mind. The mind can investigate but cannot give you the sense of truth. The *seeking* of truth, however, is an activity that is oriented in the mind.

So the truth is here, but you are looking somewhere else. You might even find the truth, the essential aspect of Truth, but that is not exactly what will give you release. It is tricky to get to the third solution because if you are trying to get to the release, you are using the first two attitudes. The third strategy in the story is not trying to achieve any results. Achieving results is still the movement of the first two strategies. The common element in the first two solutions is not the pain or pleasure, but a certain movement that is goal oriented. There is a desire to reach a certain goal and a movement toward it. It is the movement of desire that actually creates the pain. If you're trying to get to a goal, you're not accepting the truth as it is presented to you at the moment. Seeking the truth is the same movement. But the *spirit of truth* seems to have something to do with joy, as the story indicates. "They seemed to have endured much, but their faces were shining with joy." We want to understand how the spirit of truth connects with joy.

The story is told about Jesus. Let's remember some other things about Jesus that are relevant to this story and might help us find the meaning of the spirit of truth. What was it Jesus said about the Kingdom of Heaven? That you have to be like a little child to enter the Kingdom of Heaven. Maybe we can also learn something from little children about the spirit of truth. Little children have a certain relationship to truth that has joy in it.

What does it mean to say we must be like little children? Children jump and play around and are curious. When you see a child being curious, what do you see? What are they doing? They're learning, looking. It's a little like a person seeking truth, isn't it? Children do it in a lively way, quite fully. They're spontaneous, joyful. They're dealing with the truth since truth is what's presented to them all the time. We're getting close now to the exact relationship to the truth. As you see, the children's activity is similar to what we do when we seek truth. But there is something different in their relationship to truth that brings out joy. Why? They're not interested in the pleasure/pain principle; they're not part of the first two groups. They are in the now. They are in the present. There is heart; there is joy; there is spontaneity, lightness. So we're seeing the solution here. The solution is openness, nonattachment. When children play with something, they're not attached to it. They play with it, and then they throw it away.

Contrast these two things: seeking truth for its own sake and curiosity. What's the difference? Seeking truth is goal oriented; curiosity is not goal oriented. With curiosity, you're not looking for something; you're just looking. It is exactly in the moment. The consequences are not important. We're getting all the ingredients now to develop a more exact understanding.

What is the process children are going through when they're expanding their understanding of the world? Children will take a machine, for example, and dismantle it. They want to take it all apart. A very young one will take his shit and spread it all over the place. What's happening? It is curiosity, but what more precisely is going on? Why are they doing these things?

S: They're learning.

AH: Yes, learning is happening. They are interested in learning without even thinking about it.

S: You can't ask someone who's two years old why he's doing something. He's doing it because he's doing it. There is no motivation.

AH: Right, there is no motivation. Children are always investigating the truth. Maybe it's a sexual truth: "What have you got down there? It doesn't look like mine; there's something different about it." They are total curiosity. This curiosity is spontaneous, in the present, full of joy, and not goal oriented. There is innocence, openness, discovery. They are totally absorbed in the unfoldment, and there's a sense of wonder.

S: Often they're not smiling. They don't necessarily seem to enjoy it.

AH: A sense of joy doesn't necessarily produce a smile. It transcends pleasure or pain. The point is the involvement. We said that truth is the center of the heart. What is the action of the heart?

S: Giving.

AH: Giving. What else?

S. Loving.

AH: They're loving. Okay, that's all we need to remember. Love has something to do with the heart. And joy has something to do with the heart. So we're getting closer to what's involved in curiosity. How is love connected to this?

S: They are in harmony with themselves and the universe.

AH: That's true. But they don't think of it that way. They are involved in an activity. How can we understand the essence of it? What's going on?

S: There's really a union there. There's no separation from the object or from truth.

AH: That is true. But we still haven't answered the question about love. How does love figure in? We've said that they are involved in an activity. They are investigating something. They are learning. They have an object and are completely involved with it and open to it. What do they feel about that activity when they are investigating the truth? They love it. They love the process itself. They're not interested in the truth for any purpose except that they love it. And that loving of the truth, loving the process of curiosity, is manifested as joy. There's no separation: There's truth, there's love, and there's joy. In curiosity, they're all there together. The process of dismantling the car or the doll, of tearing it apart and putting it back together, the process of looking at each other's genitals—all these they love. It's not the doll or the car or the genitals that they like so much; it's the process itself, the activity and movement. It's not oriented toward anything. It is just something going on, alive; and the movement itself is the very fact of appreciating what's happening.

What you're doing here in this group is that you're engaged in an activity. Everything is here for us to be curious about. Like the child, we can engage in a continuous process of curiosity. There's joy in that, in the activity itself. The child is not looking for happiness, not trying to avoid pain. There is just a continuous process of curiosity, and that process of curiosity is nothing but loving and feeling joy in the truth itself. It is the love of truth and the joy in finding the truth. That is the movement of curiosity. There is no way you can separate curiosity from loving the truth and the joy in discovery. As we said, seeking truth is the activity of the mind. Curiosity, on the other hand, is the activity of the heart. It is, in a sense, the mind of the heart.

So you see how the attitude of curiosity, which is called the spirit of truth, is not goal oriented. In other words, curiosity has no desire in it. It is a complete, one-hundred-percent involvement in the present. It is, itself, the freedom and the joy. When the heart is curious, there is joy.

S: Would you say that these children are doing the Work at their own level?

AH: In a sense you could say that. But they're not really working; they are living, really living.

S: But isn't that what the Work is?

AH: That's what the Work should be.

S: Doesn't it follow that the correct spirit for us to be doing this Work should be the spirit of curiosity and discovery?

AH: Yes, that's what I'm saying. A central, crucial aspect of this Work is curiosity. That is the method, the goal, and the path. There is no need to be enlightened to become curious. Curiosity is an attitude that we're capable of at any time. It is curiosity that opens the joy. Joy is curiosity. As you love the truth, or as truth loves the activity you are engaged in, truth shines. That shining of the truth is the joy. You are being the truth, investigating the truth, loving the truth, and your joy is joy in the truth.

The most exact definition of curiosity is "joy in the truth," or "the joy of the truth." It is the joy of the heart, the love of the heart. As you can see, it is very, very different from the attitudes of the first two groups in our story. Curiosity transcends but does not reject pain. That is why it says in the story, "they endured much." There is pain, but "their faces shone with joy." Pain doesn't have to go. You can enjoy investigating it. You are as curious about pain as you are about pleasure.

"Oh, look at this wonderful thing! Orange and yellow and gold and red, and oh, it feels wonderful and exciting, and look what it is, what it's doing to my genitals! Oh, it feels so good! Isn't that interesting? What makes it feel so good? Well, look at that! This color makes me feel this way, this one makes me feel that way. Now, let me put them together. Oh, now it's totally different!"

You see, it's totally in the now. Curiosity cannot be in the future. You can be curious about the past or the future, but curiosity is a process in the present that involves appreciating what you experience right at this moment.

So curiosity, or the spirit of truth, is not just seeking the truth; it is not a goal-oriented activity. When the child is seeking truth by dismantling a doll, this is not time-oriented seeking. There is a joy in every second. The activity itself is full of aliveness, excitement, sensation, appreciation. It's as if you put all of yourself in one point—mind, heart, sensation.

I think this should be the main principle of our lives because when we are curious we are completely whole, happy. We are doing what we are made to do. We are not engaging in the things that bring us more and more suffering and frustration. We are engaged in something that frees the heart and mind without even seeking that freedom. The process itself is the freedom. You are free every moment that you are completely curious. Whatever happens to be there, you're in love with it. You're completely in love with yourself, with your existence. You're completely in love with whatever is presented to you. You love it so much that you want to know everything about it.

S: About children: if they're allowed to act on their curiosity, they are so often cruel, destructive, even self-destructive.

AH: That is not our concern now. Children have all kinds of other forces operating in them—sadism, aggression, all kinds of things. Today we're talking about curiosity. If children had only curiosity and nothing else, the personality would not develop. We will talk about these other factors in time. For now, talking about curiosity might bring up some fear in us, some issues about how we see children behaving in other ways, even fears about the idea of "unbridled curiosity." That's fine. We could investigate those fears, become curious about them.

I'm saying this today because it's important for many students. If you are oriented in the Work towards getting good things and getting rid of bad things, you will continue suffering. You will not understand the spirit of the Work, the spirit of truth. But if you are curious, it doesn't matter if there is pain sometimes. Joy is not the absence of suffering. Joy is the presence of curiosity. It is the presence of discovery. Then you can see not just the Work, not just your effort, but all of existence as a beautiful, intricate, exquisite field. This beauty, this magnificence, includes everything in it, including ugliness. You can see an ugliness so ugly that it is beautiful, because you are seeing the truth. The truth is what makes things beautiful.

Curiosity leads to the truth without being oriented by the personality. Curiosity is the motivation from Essence itself. Paradoxically, the first thing we need to do is not to seek curiosity. The point is to *investigate* curiosity, to become curious about curiosity. It is something that cannot be sought, just like happiness can't be sought. You seek happiness, and you kill it. You seek curiosity, and you kill it. So just observe your moments of curiosity. Be curious about them; see how there is joy there. Joy is the flicker, the spark of curiosity. It is the spark of truth operating. Curiosity is not seeking; it is living.

SEVENTEEN

Gathering Honey

There was a secret Work school that existed in Afghanistan for thousands of years called "Sarmoun Darq," which means "The Beehive" or the "Collectors of Honey." The purpose of this beehive was to collect human knowledge during the times when knowledge was dissipating and store it for future times when it could be used again. Most often undertaken in times of difficulty on earth, times of turmoil or war, this activity is so profound that most people cannot even conceive of what is involved and what significance it has.

When we say the Sarmoun Darq stores human knowledge, we do not mean information. Information can be collected in books. There is no need to form a school or a secret society to store information. Unlike information, this knowledge is material in the way that honey is material. The knowledge is actually collected in the same way that bees collect nectar from flowers and change it into honey. This is why the school is called The Beehive; its function is to collect all kinds of nectars—aspects of essential knowledge. The members have the capacity to concentrate it and change all the aromatic, beautiful nectars into very thick, sweet honey which they can then store in special flasks. When the right time comes, the flasks are opened and the knowledge is given out according to what is needed.

The nectars are the different aspects of knowledge about Essence, and the honey is the distilled pure knowledge of Essence. The image of the bees and the honey and the hive and the nectar is the closest description of the actual reality of the school. It is the closest description of the actual reality because knowledge of Essence *is* material that can be collected, concentrated, and distilled. This becomes obvious when we understand that Essence actually exists just as honey exists, just as nectars exist. The real knowledge about Essence is Essence itself. Essence is itself the knowledge.

This school, the Sarmoun Darq, collects the human Essence during difficult times on earth and stores it in special flasks. These special flasks are actually carefully prepared human beings. In this way, knowledge is preserved and passed on to other flasks until it is needed. Then these flasks, these human containers, are sent to different places to give out a particular material, material of whatever density or profundity can be absorbed.

If you look at any Work system, Work group, or Work school from the deepest, most direct, most obvious, most phenomenological point of view, you see their work is simply collecting, distilling, and purifying human Essence so that it becomes as concentrated as possible in the human individual. This is done by whatever techniques the group or school has at that time. They use in this activity whatever method they have at their disposal. Like bees changing pollen to honey, the members collect nectars and transform them into human Essence for themselves and for everybody else. The particular activity depends on the person in charge of the school who prescribes the method which the members of the group use, each person according to her own capacity. Often, most of the people don't even know exactly what they are doing. They only know the activity; they do not know all that it can accomplish. In time, as we have seen in the work we do here, people begin to understand more and more what it is they are actually doing.

At the beginning, people will see that they are looking at their emotions. They're sensing, looking, and listening, observing their reactions, understanding their patterns. After doing that for a while, they start seeing the connections between these emotions and the loss of various aspects of their essence. As that loss is felt, Essence is present more and more in the person.

In the work we do here, everybody works individually most of the time, either in private sessions or within a group context. Everyone is doing his share of collecting the nectars, of whatever quality and density he can collect. Then it is necessary for everybody to get together and engage in a certain activity that, at its deepest level, is the gathering of these nectars in one place, so that by a certain process, the nectar can be purified and distilled, made as concentrated as possible. This is the product of the work of the weekend. Specifically, it is the function of the Sunday afternoon work period. It is not just the end of the weekend; it is a time when all the work that has been done since our last meeting is present in one place. Its intensity has developed over the weekend, and everybody has done his or her part. Then we all get together and do certain things so that what has been collected can jell. Essence is then present in ways that are much more palpable, much more defined.

Each weekend brings out a different quality. And each aspect of Essence becomes clearer, more palpable, more purified, more concentrated. In this way, everybody can taste what it is like.

That is the most profound level of the work. The particular activity that we do here on Sunday afternoons is to practice being fully present, as fully present as we can be, while we engage in physical activities such as gardening, painting, and so forth. You sense, look, and listen with whatever essential capacity you have, in whatever activity or task you are doing. This activity both facilitates the function I've just described and enables you to practice being present in an atmosphere and place where this is encouraged. The presence of many people engaged in the same task adds energy. This energy is not just additive. The presence of Essence is contagious, and since everybody is sensing, looking, and listening intensely while they are working on the tasks, it is possible to create a certain amount of honey in more concentrated form than is possible at other times. So sensing, looking, and listening will give each person an added capacity to be present and will help each person taste the honey. Each of you can then take this taste of Essence and the capacity to be present back into your life. In time, you can take it into your life more and more so that your life increasingly becomes the essential life.

These methods are scientific. When you do them, you achieve precise results. If they are not followed, something else results. It is much easier for many bees to make honey than for just one bee to attempt it. One bee by itself won't make honey. It will die very quickly. You never see a bee with its own hive making honey. This example of the ancient school of the Sarmoun Darq illustrates the kind of thing that we are doing here.

The Diamond Approach is taught by Ridhwan teachers, certified by the Ridhwan Foundation. Ridhwan teachers are also ordained ministers of the Ridhwan Foundation. They are trained by DHAT Institute, the educational arm of the Ridhwan Foundation, through an extensive seven-year program, which is in addition to their work and participation as students of the Diamond Approach. The certification process ensures that each person has a good working understanding of the Diamond Approach and a sufficient capacity to teach it before being ordained and authorized to be a Ridhwan teacher.

The Diamond Approach described in this book is taught in group and private settings in California and Colorado by Ridhwan teachers.

For information, write:

> Ridhwan
> P.O. Box 10114
> Berkeley, California 94709-5114

> Ridhwan School
> P.O. Box 18166
> Boulder, Colorado 80308–8166

Satellite groups operate in other national and international locations. For information about these groups, or to explore starting a group in your area, taught by certified Ridhwan teachers, write:

> Ridhwan
> P.O. Box 10114
> Berkeley, California 94709-5114

Diamond Approach is a registered service mark of the Ridhwan Foundation.